The Soul of the Salesman

The Soul of the Salesman

The Moral Ethos of Personal Sales

Guy Oakes

Humanities Press International, Inc.
New Jersey and London

First published 1990 by Humanities Press International, Inc.
Atlantic Highlands, N.J., and 3 Henrietta Street, London WC2E 8LU.

© Guy Oakes, 1990

Library of Congress Cataloging–in–Publication Data
Oakes, Guy.
   The soul of the salesman : the moral ethos of personal sales/Guy
Oakes.
     p. cm.
   Includes bibliographical references.
   ISBN 0–391–03682–3   ISBN 0–391–03683–1 (pbk.)
   1. Sales personnel—Training of. 2. Selling—Moral and ethical
aspects I. Title.
HF5439.8.035   1990
658.8′5—dc20

                                          90–31350
                                              CIP

British Cataloguing in Publication Data
Oakes, Guy
   The soul of the salesman : the moral ethos of personal sales.
   1. United States. Salesmanship
   I. Title
   658.850973

ISBN 0–319–03682–3
ISBN 0–319–03683–1 pbk

Printed in the United States of America

In Memory of Esther H. Brown

Contents

Acknowledgments

For material on training programs in the life insurance industry, thanks are due to Eugene O'Hara and David Rinsky (The Prudential). Andrew Grossman and Arthur Vidich read sections of an earlier draft of this project and offered useful suggestions for their improvement. Research was supported by the Jack T. Kvernland Chair, Monmouth College, N.J.

This book is dedicated to my maternal grandmother. Her conversation, card games, fried chicken, apple pie, peach cobbler, leisurely country breakfasts, and running commentaries on radio serials remain among the fondest memories of my early youth in the rural Midwest. Following the untimely death of her husband during the Depression, she worked as a trainer of saleswomen for household goods. Covering territory in the South and the Midwest in a Chevrolet coupe, she always kept ready at hand a sand-filled leather cosh and a .22 Colt revolver under the roadmaps on her carseat.

1

Introduction: The Moral Arena of Personal Sales

THE SALES PROCESS

Training in personal sales—from cosmetics, vacuum cleaners, and real estate to mutual funds, higher education, and life insurance—is based on the assumption that the salesperson is made and not born. Selling is an acquired skill, proficiency in which results from the mastery of principles and techniques that are formulated in training programs, inculcated by trainers, and applied by the sales force in the field. On the one hand, it is clear that the repudiation of this assumption would result in the collapse of a substantial sector of the service industry—the armies of lecturers, consultants, and authors who market their alleged expertise in training sales personnel. On the other hand, this consideration does not entail that the assumption itself should be dismissed as nothing more than the cynical and self-serving rhetoric of the occupational group that exploits it as an ideology and lives off the benefits produced by its acceptance. On the contrary, commitment to this assumption in the personal sales industry is universal and unconditional. As a result, the assumption is more firmly grounded in the culture of the industry than even its most unrestrained enthusiasts would have us believe.

Marketing executives conceive of sales within the framework of sales training programs: as a differentiated and graduated process of recruiting prospects and enlisting referrals, conducting sales interviews, closing sales, and servicing clients. Sales managers subject their trainees to the disciplines of these programs: the convincing performance of "field tested," tried and true sales tracks and scripts; the versatile use of the telephone as a sales instrument through the practice of "smiling and dialing"; and the mastery

1

of impression management and role playing that forges the personality of the salesperson into a highly refined tool of marketing strategy. Sales managers also impose on their forces the various performance criteria and quotas specified in the programs: weekly minima of "cold" calls completed, prospects contacted, referred leads pursued, sales interviews conducted, and "closes" consummated. And perhaps most important, sales personnel not only tolerate intrusive surveillance and rigorous control of their everyday lives by sales managers. They also subject themselves to a constant daily regimen of self-scrutiny in order to produce a comprehensive and systematic self-assessment of their performance in light of the expectations of the programs.

Because of the socialization processes and social control mechanisms they set in motion, training programs in personal sales have an institutional prominence that cannot be exaggerated. The strategies set out in these programs do not merely define and regulate the sales process and control the performance of the sales force. They also form the occupational identity of sales personnel by specifying how selling is to be understood, analyzed, and assessed. In personal sales, knowledge is power. What constitutes sales, what qualifies as success and failure in the execution of the sales process, and what it means to be a salesperson are all determined by the principles of the training programs.

In the personal sales industry, the preeminence of these principles is demonstrated most dramatically in the annual ritual performed to honor the highest performers in the sales force and celebrate their achievement: the company convention. Conventions are generally held either in a major city, featuring tourist attractions and prime shopping opportunities for the daytime amusement of spouses and children, or at a "mega-resort" in locations such as Lake Tahoe in California, Kiawah Island off the coast of South Carolina, or the eight-hundred-acre Westin resort on the Hawaiian island of Kawai, which advertises "10 miles of waterways (complete with gondolas and outrigger canoes), 8 miles of paths for horse-drawn carriages, 11 restaurants, and the largest swimming pool in the islands, which is fed by four waterfalls."[1] Warm-water resorts and winter conventions are, of course, the favored combination. The company books ample blocks of space in new hotels. Successful performers and their families receive spacious and impressively appointed quarters. Luxurious "theme suites" with fresh flowers, imported champagnes, and other accessories are reserved for higher achievers. The top performers may be diverted with more exotic accommodations and perquisites: a flight to Tangier, Bangkok, or Hong Kong; extravagant suites with marble bathrooms; lavish gifts such as porcelain tea sets and silk robes; daily fashion shows; and, for the highest producer, the $13,500 gold-and-diamond Rolex watch and a $6,500 mink for his wife.[2]

Plenary sessions are held in massive convention spaces that can be quickly transformed into Las Vegas-like entertainment facilities, with vast ballrooms, huge video screens, and the latest in audiovisual technology. Everything is new, slick, and clean, exhibiting the efficiency and flawlessly managed order that the company hopes to project to its sales force. Although immense salary differentials and differences in status are represented by the participants in these conferences, both business and entertainment are transacted on a first-name basis—from the bottom of the organization and the newest recruits whose performance qualifies them for first-time attendance, to the senior luminaries of the company and the CEO himself. Codes of dress are also considerably more relaxed and individualistic than the regulations that hold in company sales offices. With plaids and checks, polyester and leisure suits, two shades of pastel, and two-tone shoes much in evidence, the dress-for-success aesthetic seems to be suspended on these occasions.

The main purpose of the convention is to recharge the energies and pump up the egos of sales personnel, to inspire the sales force to ever higher levels of achievement. In the unlikely event that the accommodations and facilities of the convention center are not adequate to realize this purpose, no matter. Convention organizers, who specialize in planned spontaneity, arrange programs designed to fabricate excitement. The resulting mood suggests a somewhat forced and synthetic enthusiasm, perhaps approximating the emotional state that the sociologist Georg Simmel called sterile excitation. Short blocks of time in business are reserved for brief speeches by upper-level managers from the home office. These remarks are intended to increase the self-esteem of sales personnel, a part of their equipment likely to be severely battered after a year of rough treatment at the hands of boorish and recalcitrant prospects. In documenting the size and traditions of the company, its impressively diversified holdings and professionally managed portfolio of investments, company officers encourage sales personnel to identify themselves with the prestige claimed by the company and link their fate with what is represented as a major growth industry. These exquisitely choreographed presentations are served up with an assortment of company-commissioned videos, often of commercial television quality and set against the background of upbeat but unobtrusive white-disco music. Videos almost invariably include footage featuring new corporate headquarters, recent acquisitions, and high-profile photo-opportunities of company officers pictured with corporate or political leaders who enjoy instant name recognition. Final scenes are generally devoted to a few select members of the sales force: unusually successful performers of recent years and their families, captured in some "world-class" resort playground, enjoying the fruits of their commissions.

However, prime time on the speaker's platform tends to be reserved for speakers who can "excite" the audience, "excitement" and its cognates being favored expressions at these assemblages. Speakers may be drawn from the company's peak performers, its leaders and stars. Or the company may bring in experts in sales technique who enjoy an industry-wide recognition based on best-selling, how-to-succeed books and national exposure on the lecture and seminar circuit. Speakers may also include national figures who have achieved media attention and fame in any legally respectable enterprise: athletic coaches with brilliant records, former astronauts, CEOs legendary for their charismatic leadership qualities, corporate take-over artists, real estate tycoons, military officers with a reputation for heroism and toughness, or former POWs celebrated in the public consciousness for their famous escapes—demonstrating that even under the most adverse conditions imaginable, sheer will, perseverance, and sound training will carry the day.

Speakers break the ice with sports humor and develop their presentations with metaphors drawn from athletics, especially baseball and American football, taking advantage of the fact that on the whole their audience is made up of avid sports fans and passionate consumers of sports as entertainment. If they arrive well-briefed, they also know that sales personnel are taught to translate the ideology of sports into an occupational ethic: in the end, hard work and training in the basics produce victory. The ultimate purpose of these inspirational talks by super salesmen or their surrogates is to reinforce the doctrine that even the highest paid performers achieve their results by applying the simplest principles of sales training programs: setting goals that are challenging but not unreasonable; fashioning the plans required to reach these goals; and acquiring the training and practicing the skills essential to the execution of these plans. Sales personnel who draw the appropriate conclusions can expect that if they follow the same strategies that produced the stellar performances represented on the platform or the screen, then one day they too will find their place on the dais reserved for industry leaders.

THE PARADOXES OF PERSONAL SALES

This study focuses on a twofold question: How do training programs in personal sales define the sales process and, as a consequence of this definition, how is the identity of the salesperson formed? In chapters 2 and 3, I demonstrate the bipolar character of the sales process and the dual identity of the salesperson. Training programs define the sales process, but in a contradictory fashion, by employing two antithetical conceptual and rhetorical idioms. As a result, sales and selling are conceived of as two quite different modes of interaction, constituted by opposing purposes and controlled by conflicting sets of rules. Put another way, training programs in personal sales school sales personnel in the methods by which they can expect to succeed. However, the lesson they teach is not unequivocal. On the contrary, it is articulated in two conflicting modes of discourse that encode, systematize, and regulate the practice of sales on the basis of mutually inconsistent assumptions.

In one mode of discourse, the sales process is conceived of as a strategic interaction that typically involves a contest between salesperson and prospect. The purpose of this contest is to maximize the salesperson's commissions on sales. In order to achieve this objective, it is necessary to break down the suspicion, indifference, fear, or antagonism of the prospect. Sales personnel never take "no" for an answer, nor do they even regard a negative response as a refusal. Every "no" is a potential tactic to be employed to the salesperson's advantage in the struggle for the commitment of the prospect. Armed with the techniques of their training, sales personnel attempt to move the prospect—carefully, respectfully, even sympathetically, but nevertheless unyieldingly—to the final payoff, the close. This view represents both the sales process and the sales personnel in the terms of a commercial idiom. The ultimate concern of sales is not the product or service offered for sale. In the final analysis, sales is about the prospect's money. The purpose of sales is to get as much of it as possible. The prospect is a means to this end, an instrument of the sales process.

In the other mode of discourse, the sales process is understood as the performance of a service. The prospect is regarded not as a potential antagonist who is manipulated to generate commissions, but as a client whose needs are paramount in the transaction. Because sales personnel are conceived of as service professionals who offer their expertise to clients, their performance is controlled by rules that govern professional conduct and require a respect for the client's autonomy and integrity. This view represents the sales process and sales personnel in the terms of a service idiom. The ultimate concern of sales is not the income of the salesperson, but the welfare of the client. In the final analysis, sales is about clients and their needs. The purpose of sales is to meet these needs as effectively as possible. The salesperson is a means to this end, an instrument of the sales process.

This account of the sales process and sales personnel seems paradoxical. How can the ruthless gamester also qualify as the caring service professional? How can a role defined in purely commercial terms also be governed by a professional ethic? How can performances assessed solely on the basis of cost/benefit criteria also be expected to measure up to the standards of a service ideal? In chapter 4, I address these questions by arguing that the definition of the sales process on the basis of a commercial idiom and a service idiom generates a number of antinomies. The identity of sales personnel is framed by the paradoxes entailed by these antinomies. As a result, the role of the salesperson is defined in contradictory terms.

How can sales personnel come to terms with the stresses and pressures produced by fundamental conflicts between the commercial idiom and the service idiom? What possible interpretations can be placed on these antinomies and paradoxes by anyone capable of measuring up to the competitive demands of a career in personal sales? In chapter 5, I examine the status of these contradictions in the work world of personal sales, and explore the means by which their impact on the performance of the sales force is diminished.

A note on the concept of personal sales, which in the textbook literature on marketing and sales is generally understood as designating any face-to-face contact between salesperson and customer.[3] In the ensuing analysis, personal sales will be construed somewhat more narrowly. Face-to-face interaction between a salesperson and a potential customer will be understood as falling under the concept of personal sales only if the interaction itself is governed by the multiphased sales process: the several steps of recruiting and qualifying prospects, interviewing potential customers, closing the sale, and servicing clients. This means that a comprehensive range of sales positions will not be considered in this investigation. They include the following: sales personnel whose primary function is to deliver merchandise; sales clerks who work in retail stores and may not even have occasion to speak to customers; retail sales personnel who take orders, close sales, and provide services, but are not responsible for prospecting; wholesalers whose main function is to call on businesses that retail the goods in their inventory and insure that this stock of goods is maintained at a level sufficient to accommodate consumer demand; "missionary" sales personnel, who are not expected to make sales or even take orders, but only to educate the customer—usually a retailer—concerning a line of products or build good will on behalf of a marketing organization; and finally, technical, industrial, or institutional sales personnel who function mainly as advisors or consultants to clients. In sum, personal sales is defined by the sales process, and it can be said that sales personnel are engaged in personal sales only if the interaction between salesperson and consumer is controlled by the principles that govern the performance of this process.

There is perhaps a temptation to further restrict the concept of personal sales so that it is limited to transactions in which prospects act on their own behalf and not as representatives of a company or as professional experts. In the language of the law of agency, it would follow that in personal sales the prospect functions as a principal, not as an agent. Given this proviso, it could be said that the salesperson and the prospect confront one another directly. Their interaction is not mediated by the interest of a company or a client that the prospect represents, nor does it depend upon the status the prospect may have as a representative of a company or a client. This, it might be said, is what makes the sale personal: the salesperson sells to the personal and private needs of prospects, not to impersonal corporate or professional interests for which prospects may speak in their occupational role. From the standpoint of the sales process, this is a distinction without a difference. In personal sales, the same principles and strategies obtain regardless of whether the salesperson sells to the personal, corporate, or professional interests of the prospect. The same techniques and skills apply independent of the question of whether the prospect enters the interaction as a principal or as an agent representing other interests. Put in more concrete terms, from the perspective of the sales process, there is no difference in principle between selling an automobile to a prospect as a private individual and selling the same vehicle to the same prospect as a purchasing agent of a taxicab fleet, or between selling a mutual fund to a prospect as a private investor and selling it to the same prospect as the manager of a pension fund.

Finally, personal sales should not be conflated with the direct sales techniques employed by companies such as Mary Kay Cosmetics, Amway, Tupperware, or the A. C. Williams insurance organization. Conceptually, direct sales falls under the more general category of personal sales. As a type of personal sales, it is distinguished by two additional features. First, the locus of the sale is usually the prospect's home, not the salesperson's office or any other place of business. Second, the organizational status of sales personnel is distinctive in the following respect: salespersonnel are not employees of the company whose products they market, but are independent contractors who buy wholesale the products that they sell directly to consumers.[4]

THE SOCIOLOGY OF SALES

As F. William Howton and Bernard Rosenberg observed twenty-five years ago, social scientists have demonstrated a curious indifference to sales personnel, a tendency that has not changed substantially in the last quarter-century.[5] There is, of course, a massive literature on blue collar workers, the history of working-class movements, and the culture of the industrial workplace.[6] In addition, public and private bureaucracies and the work of white collar employees have provided the primary data for the investigation of formal organizations.[7] A remarkable range of service industry occupations—from ambulance drivers, clerical workers, and Chinese laundrymen to cocktail waitresses and airline attendants—has also been studied intensively.[8] The sociology of professions has developed not only detailed analyses of virtually every profession, but also a battery of competing theories of professionalization, its causes and consequences.[9] And most recently, the social world of the modern corporation and its various levels of managerial personnel have been thoroughly surveyed.[10] In comparison with the comprehensive range of research pursued on these occupational groups, the social structure of sales organizations, the operation of these organizations, the work world of sales personnel, and the place of sales in the mass retail economy and the consumer culture of the twentieth century remain virtually unchartered territory. In light of the attention lavished on other occupational strata, the relative dearth of research in the sociology of sales is difficult to account for. It is especially remarkable in view of the pervasive use of sales strategies in all spheres of modern life and the impact of the moral ethos of sales on a world in which all values appear to be negotiable and everything seems to be for sale.

If there is a received sociological perspective on personal sales, it is enunciated most clearly in C. Wright Mills' famous essay, "The Great Salesroom."[11] This perspective is theoretically unproductive and, at least for the post-World War II history of sales, empirically out of date. "The Great Salesroom" is limited to an examination of the social organization of retail sales in the large urban department store based on the model of Macy's. Mills stresses the alleged exploitation and depersonalization of sales personnel, which he regards as a consequence of the forces of managerial capitalism. He ignores the creation and institutionalization of new skills and techniques produced by the socialization of sales personnel in industry training programs. Mills' highly impressionistic observations do not qualify as an analysis of the modern sales process. They serve rather as putative illustrations of his own theory of the new middle class, its dispositions and mentalities. Driven by the pursuit of prestige, riven by status consciousness and envy, under Mills' Balzacian eye, the salesperson is merely another example of the alienated and expropriated personality fabricated by the demands of the mass retail economy, the oversupply of goods and services, and the need to stimulate new demand at every point of distribution. The logic of the sales process and the manner in which it forms a distinctive type of human being with characteristic skills and techniques are ignored in favor of a reductive and mechanical application of Marxist slogans to the world of sales as Mills conceives it.

It is obvious that the several industries generally included under the rubric of personal sales cannot be handled responsibly in a single study. In the ensuing, I attempt to support the above claims by analyzing contemporary life insurance sales. It was the life insurance industry that first introduced and institutionalized training programs for sales forces.[12] The sheer size of the industry, its importance in modern life—from a source of minimal financial security for families to a base of large-scale capital investment for corporations—and the legions of agents it places in the field make life insurance a major consumer of sales training programs. The Life Insurance Marketing and Research Association (LIMRA) estimates that between 1973 and 1988, the amount of money the American public spent on financial security in both public and private programs increased from twenty-four percent to thirty-two percent of disposable income. Of this increase, sixty percent has been devoted either to life insurance (twelve percent) or to retirement plans (forty-eight percent), which are also marketed by life insurance companies. Life insurance is virtually universal in American households with incomes exceeding $20,000. Even eighty percent of families with incomes that fall between $15,000 and $20,000 are covered by some form of life insurance. According to LIMRA calculations, in 1988, 239,900 full-time life insurance agents were active in the field. The average agent with at least five years' experience sold fifty-five life insurance policies worth $3,716,000, with total premiums to the company issuing the policy valued at $47,380. These figures indicate an estimate of $11.37 billion in total earnings for the industry from life insurance policies sold in 1988 alone. LIMRA also estimates that at the beginning of 1986, thirty-five new agents were hired for every one hundred agents under contract. If this ratio also held for 1988, then in that year, the industry recruited 83,965 new agents who became candidates for training.[13]

The life insurance industry is also a major producer of training programs in sales, which may be classified under four headings. (1) The largest companies produce their own programs, either by using in-house specialists who work in the sales and marketing research staff of the company or by employing consultants who design a "unique" program customized to the needs and image of the company. (2) Smaller companies use generic programs developed by consultants, who are frequently agents with legendary sales records and industry-wide prestige. (3) LIMRA, the official marketing research organization of the industry, provides a full line of training materials and services that are available to companies, agencies, and individual agents. (4) Finally, industry trade journals regularly feature articles on sales training for both trainees as well as established agents who feel it is time to sharpen their skills. This study draws on material from each of these sources, which form the primary data of the investigation.

A secondary source of data is provided by a collection of seventy-four interviews conducted in 1987–89. The interviewees were mainly life insurance agents with territories between New York City and Philadelphia. Also interviewed were general agents—the managers of regional agencies of specific insurance companies—and their sales managers, both of whom are responsible for training agents. Finally, consultants who specialize in lectures and seminars in all fields of personal sales were interviewed. Initial interviews generally lasted from one hour to ninety minutes. From the original group of seventy-four interviewees, thirty-two were interviewed a second time. From this second group, fifteen were interviewed repeatedly and more intensively over the two year period. The fifteen agents in this last group worked for a variety of life insurance companies. Some had only a few months in the business, others more than twenty-five years. They also represented quite different levels of success in the industry. While some had been terminated by more than one company, others were major producers or "heavy hitters," members of the Million Dollar Roundtable and active in the National Association of Life Underwriters. An additional set of twenty-five interviews was conducted at a national company convention, where I was able to speak with agents from other parts of the United States. These were brief, somewhat fugitive, and frequently impromptu encounters, usually of fifteen to thirty minutes in duration.

Collecting this second source of data proved to be a frustrating but not unenlightening exercise. At the outset of my research, I attempted to gain permission from several large life insurance companies to participate in the training programs required of new recruits. Without knowing it at the time, I was following the "referred lead" strategy favored in the personal sales industry, building and setting in motion an elaborate set of contacts that would vouch for my *bona fides* and eventually provide access to the company officials who control entry to training programs. After constructing these routes to general agents, sales vice presidents, and vice presidents for district and regional agencies, I found that all my efforts were rebuffed. Requests for permission to attend sales conferences for general agents and sessions on sales techniques for sales managers proved no more successful. However, in establishing these contacts, I became acquainted with a number of agents and consultants who not only agreed to be interviewed, but also introduced me to other agents who proved willing. In this unplanned and piecemeal fashion, a body of interviewees was built up.

Interviewees seemed motivated in part by a limited curiosity about the project and in part by more robust considerations: an interest in forming yet another contact who might be able to provide them with business. In the latter case, the agents and I attempted to make use of one another, in both instances for the purpose of extracting impressions, information, and especially new names, an irony that escaped me at the time. Surprisingly, no one tried to persuade me to buy life insurance, nor did the question of my own financial security needs ever come up. However, a number of agents made efforts to use me as a source of referred leads and encouraged me to provide them with the names, addresses, phone numbers, and personal financial data of colleagues who had money problems, money to invest, or new financial obligations. As we shall see, failure to do so would have amounted to a gross violation of the norms governing the sales process in which these agents were trained.

As is often the case in ethnography, many interviewees could not or would not speak candidly in response to questions from an outsider, especially when the issues touched on the meaning and value of their work. Other agents spoke more freely, providing useful perspectives that supplemented, confirmed, or called into question conclusions drawn from the basic data of industry training programs. All interviews with agents active in the industry were conducted on the condition of anonymity. Accordingly, the names of agents and companies that appear in the interviews reported below are fictions. Interviews were taped on a hand-held microcassette recorder and transcribed by the author.

A few of the interviews took place in agents' offices. The majority were conducted either at Monmouth College or, most frequently, in the field: in restaurants, bars, and coffee shops, waystations to which agents repair when they find themselves between calls to prospects. As the ensuing analysis shows, the success of agents depends upon their ability to market trust in their own probity. Prospects will buy a policy only if they first buy the trustworthiness of the agent. This is why successful agents always attempt to sell themselves and their integrity before they try to sell a product. My limited experience in exploring the occupational lives of life insurance agents suggests that although they live off the trust they inspire in others, they are extremely parsimonious in the investment of their own trust. As one agent put it, with an excess that is typical of the industry: "In this business, you don't trust anybody." Everyone, it seems, has an angle, a hidden agenda, and ulterior motives that are probably base, indefensible, and calculated to thwart the agent's own interests. It is hardly astonishing that this mentality leads agents to be suspicious and cynical about declarations of intention and statements of purpose. Nor under these circumstances is it surprising that my own motives for interviewing agents were often construed in pecuniary rather than scholarly terms. Thus I was frequently suspected of compiling data for yet another expose of the life insurance industry or of gathering material for a bestseller that would represent agents as frauds, cheats, and charlatans. Such, however, is not the case. Readers seeking new recommendations for the regulation or reform of the life insurance industry will not find them here.

THE SOCIOLOGY OF COMMERCIAL ETHICS

This study analyzes various aspects of the moral ethos of life insurance sales and examines some of the ethical problems posed by the sales process in which agents are trained. However, it does not pass moral judgments on the activities under investigation, nor does it offer ethical approbation or blame concerning any practice in which agents engage or any technique they employ. The author does not write as an "ethicist," and repudiates any claim to whatever special competence this species of intellectual may reserve to itself. Nor should this study be identified with recent fashions in academic "business ethics," which extract ethical theories from the philosophical tradition, fine-tune them in the workshops of contemporary philosophy professors, and apply them to the moral evaluation of current business practices. Readers interested in an ethical assessment of the life insurance industry or a moral critique of life insurance sales are advised to look elsewhere. The territory of this report—its questions, analyses, and conclusions—lies not within the realm of ethical judgment, but rather in the sociology of ethics.

Construed most narrowly, this study investigates the training programs in which American life insurance agents learn their metier, and explores some of the moral conflicts these programs generate. Viewed more broadly, it analyzes several aspects of the moral culture of personal sales in contemporary American life. Conceived most generously, it sketches certain features of the commercialization of American life, their meaning, and their consequences. Thus, in certain respects, this investigation depicts the way we live now. The strategies and techniques institutionalized in the personal sales industry—from the use of the telephone as an instrument of interpersonal domination to the tactics of impression management and the development of skills in the interpretation and control of "nonverbal communication" or "body language"—have penetrated everyday life, as well as the practices of occupational groups not conventionally perceived as engaged in sales. If this study can claim a relevance beyond the limited scope of the data it analyzes, that is because the microsocial frames of contemporary life form a world of sales presentations in which someone is typically attempting to close a sale on someone else.

2

The Commercial Idiom

THE ORGANIZATION OF LIFE INSURANCE SALES

A life insurance company is organized so that the agent is the only member of the organization who has direct contact with the consumer. The role of the agent is grounded in a twofold function that is determined by the position of the agent in the company. This position is uniquely situated at the intersection of two organizational tasks: a distribution function and a production function. The agent is located at the point in the organization at which the company's products—financial security policies and plans—are distributed to the consumer, and also at the point at which services are directly produced for the consumer. The services in question are delivered by the agent, who provides consumers with information about financial security, assists them in assessing their own financial security needs, helps them form a plan for their personal financial security, and advises them concerning the purchase of products that will best meet their needs. The ultimate objective of these services is, of course, the sale of the company's products. In the conception of the sales process that underpins training programs in life insurance sales, the distribution function depends upon the production function. The company can distribute its products only if consumers buy them, and consumers can be expected to buy life insurance only if agents sell it to them.

The dual functions of product distribution and the production of service and sales are performed by two kinds of agents, who differ in the rights, responsibilities, and benefits that tie them to the company. These agents are trained and managed in two types of organizations, which the industry designates as systems: the agency or general agency system and the brokerage system. The differences between these two types of agents and supervisory organizations are primarily determined by differences in the agent's contract with the company.

15

The career agent works as an exclusive sales representative of a given company under terms controlled by a "captive agent contract." This contract makes the agent an employee of the company. As a result, career agents have access to certain benefits, such as expense allowances, health, disability, life, and dental insurance, bonuses, and the right to participate in company contests and competitions—all based on the proviso that they maintain the level of production established by the company for its full-time agents. Career agents are "captives" in the sense that they cannot, without the consent of the company, place business with other insurance carriers. Moreover, if they fail to place business with their own company that is sufficient to meet its standards covering the annual average size, number, and quality of policies, they can generally be terminated at any time. Career agents are based in a regional agency established by the company and managed by a general agent, who is employed as a sales and office manager charged with the responsibility of transacting the company's business and maintaining its sales in a certain territory.

Brokers or independent agents, on the other hand, work as autonomous contractors. They function essentially as entrepreneurs and may have independent agent contracts with several companies. They are not employees of any company, nor do they enjoy the rights of the career agent. As a rule, companies do not specify annual minimum sales quotas for independent agents, and an agent will usually be retained in this capacity as long as the company sees an advantage in maintaining the relation; this usually means as long as the agent provides the company with some business without mishandling its clients, flagrantly violating its own regulations, committing glaring illegalities, or otherwise embarrassing the company. Some independent agents are self-employed. Others work in brokerages owned by an independent agent, who supplies the agency sales force with office space and benefits in exchange for a certain percentage of commissions. Under the latter arrangement, minima specifying the amounts and kinds of business that must be sold within a given year may also be a part of the independent agent's contract. Although both career agents and independent agents are trained in the same kinds of programs, this study focuses on the work world of the career agent.

The agent's principal source of income is the commission, which is derived from premiums that purchasers of insurance pay on their policies. Commissions differ according to the type of policy. The policy favored by agents is, of course, whole-life, which carries the highest first-year commission; although there may be some variation from company to company, in general this commission is currently set at eighty-five percent of the amount of the first-year premium. The agent who sells the policy receives fifty-five percent of the first-year premium, the general agent receives thirty percent, and the company issuing the policy receives the remaining fifteen percent. During the next five years in the life of the policy, the company generally receives ninety-two percent of the premium. The commission is only eight percent, which is divided between the agent and the general agent. When this five-year period ends, the size of the commission continues to decline. The percentage of the commission received by the general agent is called an "override." Arrangements governing overrides differ considerably from agent to agent. Consistently high producers can usually negotiate lower overrides with their general agents, thus guaranteeing a higher rate of commission.

THE ORGANIZATION OF SALES TRAINING PROGRAMS

The life insurance industry rejects the traditional conception of salesman-ship as a charismatic quality with which certain gifted persons are endowed, an idiosyncratic, irrational, and, therefore, unteachable creative knack. On the contrary, salesmanship is a set of skills that, given the proper instruc-tion, can be learned. Thus the importance of a system of training in which agents learn how to sell is obvious. Depending upon the size of the agency, new agents may be trained by the general agent, the agency sales manager, or a senior agent who has the responsibility of supervising trainees. During the initial or orientation period of training, the trainee's first task is to pass the licensing examination of the state in which the agency does business. Because state laws governing the sale of insurance differ somewhat, these examinations vary from state to state. However, since the Armstrong Commission hearings of 1905 that led to legal reforms curbing corruption and abuse in the industry, state insurance laws and licensing examinations have become progressively more uniform.[14] The main professional organi-zations of agents—such as the National Association of Life Underwriters (NALU)—have also consistently lobbied for uniform state laws. Moreover, a broadly uniform code of insurance laws is an economic necessity for the major life insurance carriers, all of which are represented by agents in virtually every state.

During the orientation period, the trainee receives instruction on how to pass the state examination, information concerning the products of the company, and training in sales technique. Prior to licensing by the state, trainees may contact prospects and interview them, but they are legally prohibited from writing business for the company and actually selling policies. However, as is usually the case in the industry, there are ways around this regulation. As a result, astute, well-connected and aggressive trainess will encounter no difficulties in selling insurance and getting paid for it. As one agent notes:

> Before I passed the state exam—for which, by the way, I studied a total of about two hours—I had a really great prospect, a relative who was ready to sign for a big policy. What did I do? I went to my sales manager and told him the story. What did he do? He had a big shit-eating grin on his face. He told me to write up the app [application] and bring it in. He signed the app, even though I was the one who did all the work. Then he cut me in on a part of the commission, whatever he wanted to give me, or maybe what he thought I deserved at the time. This sort of thing is done all the time and everybody knows about it.[15]

Following the orientation period, training programs generally divide the substance of training into two areas: product knowledge and sales. Product knowledge is concerned with the full range of financial security products marketed by the company, the various benefits they produce, how they are paid for, and the different needs and interests they are intended to address. Sales principles and practices are concerned with the strategies and tactics for marketing these products. It is in this second area that the agent-in-training learns the five essential steps of the sales process and receives instruction in how to perform each one: the initial phase of "prospecting," which includes techniques for identifying potential consumers of the products sold by the company; the second phase, "approaching" the prospect, which includes techniques for making contact with prospects and convincing them to take an interest in the company's products that is sufficiently lively to motivate them to agree to a sales interview; the third phase, interviewing, which includes techniques for conducting a tightly controlled dialogue with prospects concerning their financial security needs and their willingness to pay for products that meet these needs; the fourth phase, "closing," which includes techniques for motivating prospects to sign an application for the purchase of these products and write a check for the initial premium; and the final phase, called "service" or "servicing the client," which includes techniques to insure that the purchasers of financial security products will maintain future premium payments so that their protection will not lapse.

The training schedule is generally structured by employing modules, each of which is devoted to a particular phase of the sales process. In theory, the techniques essential to the execution of each phase are mastered before the trainee moves on to the next phase. At least in the major companies, training material for each module includes magazine-like manuals printed on slick paper and featuring copious diagrams, illustrations, and graphs; videocassettes that dramatize the skills essential to selling; and exercises by means of which trainees can monitor their own progress. Although each company that produces its own training materials stresses the novel and unique qualities of its program, in fact the principles, techniques, and even the rhetoric of these programs are standardized, not only across life insurance companies but throughout personal sales.

In working their way through the training program, new agents read the materials included in each module and view the accompanying videocassettes. They also attend lecture-demonstrations that reinforce the lessons taught in these media. In role-playing sessions—one trainee playing the prospect, another the agent—they practice the skills they have learned. Finally, they begin to employ these skills by confronting real prospects in joint field work supervised by their sales manager. Joint field work enables the manager to determine whether new agents have actually mastered the techniques essential to the execution of the sales process. At the beginning of joint field work, the experienced agent generally demonstrates the correct technique on a live prospect, and the trainee observes. Then the trainee uses this technique in dealing with the next prospect, and the sales manager monitors the trainee's performance, reinforcing the successful execution of technique, replacing inappropriate behavior, and in general serving as a good coach.

Thus the trainee learns by doing. Learning is conceived of as a product of repetition. The agent learns by repeatedly performing certain stereotypical actions in the appropriate situations. Learning is also habituation, a matter of changing old habits and acquiring new dispositions. The result is a permanent change in behavior. Because learning is habituation, the skills essential to the performance of the sales process must be practiced until they can be employed with an unstudied and effortless ease. The exercise of skill must approximate an automatic response. There is a sense in which it must be performed thoughtlessly, without deliberation or calculation. Learning as habituation is held to produce a change in "attitudes." Indeed, successful training requires a total reorientation and transformation of the mentality of the agent-in-training.

In this respect, the ideal effect of training on the new agent may be compared to Max Weber's characterization of the impact of the spirit of inner-worldly asceticism on the Puritan entrepreneur. The training program requires agents to exercise a systematic surveillance and control over the conduct of life as a whole and all of its details. Essential to this rational reconstruction of life is the willingness of agents to subject themselves to the discipline of training, in which life is conceived of as a project of rigorous self-management and regulation. The agent must conceive of his or her entire life—not merely specific episodes, activities, or aspects of behavior—as an object of methodical training, supervision, and correction. The product of this reconfiguration of life as a continuous exercise in total cognitive, emotional, and moral self-control is the fully trained agent, initially the creation and subsequently the instrument of this discipline. The discipline of training breaks down the agent into an ensemble of cognitive, emotional, and moral functions—attitudes, feelings, and obligations, all of which are subject to oversight, initially by agents' handlers and eventually by agents themselves. The training literature places special emphasis on two aspects of this process: the intensive mode of control and the minute scale of its operation, in which each aspect of the agent's life is scrutinized and reduced to its smallest manipulable parts; and the uninterrupted and unrelenting quality of the surveillance that is exercised over the agent's life. The result of the systematic regulation of life by self-imposed discipline is the inculcation of specific imperatives that function as positive and negative sanctions. Positive sanctions support the behavior required for the successful execution of the sales process. Negative sanctions proscribe behavior that jeopardizes its successful execution. Thus the sales process is not merely a strategy for selling. It is a way of life, an ethos that forms the character of the agent.

The timing of each phase of training and the duration of the training period as a whole vary, depending upon the budget that the home office and the agency have devoted to the program, the sophistication of the facilities available for training, the size of the agency, and the personal proclivities of the sales manager and the general agent. In general it can be said that during the first two weeks, new agents are assigned more or less intensive blocks of reading; they attend lectures and demonstrations; they role-play each step of the sales process and learn to improve their performance by examining videotapes of these rehearsals; and they begin supervised field work. During the first month to six weeks, the trainee engages in more directed field work and undertakes independent sales activity under the supervision of the sales manager.

PROSPECTING: LESSONS IN COMMERCIAL CASUISTRY

In life insurance, there is one rule that sales managers never let their trainees forget: sales is a people business. Agents are in the business of meeting people, and people are their inventory, like the goods on a supermarket shelf. This rule covers what is generally regarded as the most important step of the sales process: prospecting. From the standpoint of an insurance company, prospects are people who have needs that can be satisfied by the products marketed by its agents. Viable prospects must be able to pay for these products; they must meet the company's underwriting requirements that qualify them as acceptable risks; and they must be receptive to a discussion of their financial security needs with an agent. Prospecting is the activity of meeting people who satisfy these conditions and convincing them to agree to a sales interview. Although probationary agents sell eighty percent of their business to people they knew before they entered the industry, established agents with at least five years in the business sell only twenty percent of their policies to people who fall under this heading.[16] Survival in the industry depends upon increasing the size of the agent's "client base"—the pool of prospects who regularly turn to the agent for advice concerning their financial security needs. According to LIMRA research, agents with an average of twelve years' experience have an average base of four hundred clients and maintain seven hundred policies in force.[17] This client base can be built and maintained only by means of intensive and systematic prospecting. Training programs generally assume that the novice cannot survive without generating five sales per week. The average industry ratio of sales to prospecting calls approximates 1:10. This means that in any given week, the new agent must contact fifty new prospects.

What are the principles that govern prospecting? Agents are trained to be uncompromisingly opportunistic in the recruitment of prospects. Everyone is a potential prospect, and every human encounter presents opportunities for prospecting. Every social relation, every mode of social intercourse, and every interaction, be it insignificant and inconsequential or sacred and inviolable, should be exploited as a way of meeting potential prospects. The sophisticated agent's observation of the usual social amenities is never the mindless expression of civility that it seems to be. For the agent on the lookout for changes in domestic status, health, or income, "Hello, how are you?" and "How's the family?" are never mere space-fillers in polite conversation. Engagements, marriages, births, divorces, deaths, new jobs, new cars, new houses, new illnesses—all these transitions provide crucial information germane to the potential prospect's financial security.

The agent is also a passionate devotee of lists. Turn-on lists from public utility companies, welcome wagon lists, mortgage lists from real estate brokers, and real estate transfers identify new home owners. Newspaper notices of monies inherited, lawsuits won, and cash awards made identify liquid assets potentially available for financial security investments. New partnerships, promotions, buy-outs, bids won, company expansions, reorganizations, and take-overs indicate an increased demand for insurance protection on the part of key persons in business. PTA lists, school graduation lists, and high school yearbooks identify parents who need to save for higher education costs. University graduation lists identify young adults whose parents may no longer face these costs and thus may have more disposable income. Membership lists of organizations such as the Red Cross, the American Cancer Society, and the American Heart and Lung Association identify people who tend to be more conscious than others of the catastrophic effects of illness, the fragility of life, the possibility of untimely death, and above all the need to be insured against these eventualities. Membership in philanthropic organizations such as opera guilds, and library, museum, theater, symphony orchestra, or hospital associations is a good indicator of affluence, as is membership in thoroughly nonphilanthropic groups associated with prodigal consumption: elite country clubs, tennis clubs, or health clubs, and associations of aircraft, boat, or horse owners. Nor will the systematic prospector fail to exploit the public telephone directory for what one consultant delicately terms "ethnic last names that tend to be linked with affluence."

Careful agents take advantage of every relevant source of information, engage in a constant surveillance of the human material at their disposal, and develop what the training manuals call "a 24-hour awareness of what makes an individual a potential customer."[18] As a connoisseur of the flotsam and jetsam of trivial conversations and the informational effluvia of life, agents are subject to what Erving Goffman has called a "rage for connectedness."[19] Thus it should be no surprise that the agent is a compulsive joiner of all manner of organizations and a participant in all conceivable community activities, exploiting the contacts established in this way for the purpose of prospecting. As one agent notes:

This may sound silly, but my manager considered it very important for me to join community organizations and boards: Little League, PTA, school boards, hospital boards. You get your face in the local paper. You know: "Ralph Williams and what he's doing now." It tells people you're with Pilgrim Mutual. You're well-established, you're a family man, you're a part of middle class America, you're a professional, you can be trusted. This is the guy you go to for insurance. So networking yourself into all these small community organizations is very important.

This modus operandi rests on an absolute refusal to respect the functional specificity of roles. Service personnel—doctors, dentists, bankers, repair-people, the butcher, the baker—all become potential prospects. The same agent makes the following observations:

My sales manager told me it would be great if I joined a country club. Theoretically, you're sitting around having lunch at the country club. And there are lawyers, doctors, and accountants there who can introduce you to other lawyers, doctors, and accountants. You go to the country club, you play some golf or tennis with a lawyer or a doctor. You find out that the doctor is the head of a professional association of ten doctors. You know, that's a tremendous group of people to do business with. It's the idea of the country club set. People with a lot of money who can afford to belong to country clubs, because often this takes a lot of money. They're always eating lunch together, playing golf together. They do business together. It's very important for you to get to know people like this.

The list of potential prospects also includes relatives, friends, and neighbors; the friends, relatives, or associates of the agent's spouse; and former schoolmates, teachers, and lovers dredged up from the past. Even the babysitter's parents and people to whom one owes money are included in the "natural market" of the agent: the list of potential prospects who can be expected to be most accessible and least resistant to a discussion of financial security requirements.[20]

Should agents exploit family members as prospects? The question is too important to be left to the agent's sensibilities or feelings of delicacy. As agents discover quite early in their training, this is a matter on which they have virtually no choice. There are two reasons why this is the case. First, as one agent observes, the recruitment of family members as prospects may be a condition for employment.

Selling family members is a must, mainly because companies tend to demand apps even before they hire you. The company essentially blue-prints you before they hire you, and one of the ways they do this is to see if you can get them ten apps, or eight apps, or whatever. You have to get them in even before they hire you. But where do these eight apps come from? They come from your family members.

In addition, prospecting family members may be a condition for survival. Another agent describes the pressure on the trainee.

> My manager was absolutely brutal about these things. My uncle is head of an architectural firm. He has a lot of money. I get my mother to talk to the uncle. I knew my manager had his eye on this big prize. He would just pound away at me to get my uncle to sign on for major coverage. One of the ways he would do this, of course, was first to tell me I wouldn't get a paycheck unless I got X amount of apps. But at the same time—although I didn't know this—he'd be calling my uncle up saying: "Look, you know Phil's gonna fail unless we can get him some more apps." So he was attacking my uncle that way, directly. My uncle wants to help his nephew, so we end up getting a major retirement plan. My manager was ruthless in getting the new people coming in to sell their families.

The indefatigable prospector even learns to assess anonymous potential prospects in their personal absence and without the benefit of the most indirect acquaintance. This is accomplished by inferring socioeconomic status and insurance needs from publicly displayed impedimenta. The ever vigilant agent driving from one residential appointment to another uses this time for prospecting. But which houses to call upon? Look for evidence of recent arrivals (out of state license plates and home renovations), young families (bicycles, swing sets, and station wagons), and, above all, middle class affluence: "If they have a good attractive yard on the outside, you'll find that things are equally as good on the inside. That's how you can find the people who are going to pay and stay."[21]

Prospecting is an enterprise that never ends, and agents can never rest secure in the belief that their list of prospects is complete. As the agent's children advance through various schools, new prospects are found among their teachers, the parents of their friends, and the various service personnel—doctors, dentists, camp counsellors, and coaches—who serve their needs. As the agent moves from one social, civic, or religious organization to another, and as the agent's spouse progresses from one job to another, new acquaintances, sponsors, mentors, or clients are added to the list of potential prospects. Because selling depends upon prospecting, this list will end only when the agent leaves the business.

The theory of the agent as consummate prospector entails that agents cannot afford to respect persons or occasions. One frequently recommended strategy depends upon the emotional manipulation of the prospect. The technique is to identify painful emotions or powerful feelings of distress that are characteristic of members of the middle class market in which most life insurance agents work. The agent's task is to play upon these emotions, encourage their expression, and convince prospects that their feelings can be assuaged or countered only by purchasing financial security products sold by the agent. Two disturbing feelings allegedly characteristic of the emotional life of members of this market are guilt and fear; for example, a husband's guilt occasioned by the fact that he has not taken the proper steps to protect his family in the event of his death, and a wife's fear of financial disaster should she become divorced or widowed. One article on prospecting technique recommends the following double-barrelled approach that assaults both emotions simultaneously, "a personal letter" that will induce fear as well as guilt by hitting the prospect with what the author describes as "an emotional sledgehammer."[22]

Subject: Widows and divorcees hit the skids!
Dear Mr. and Mrs. Smith:
   A new statistic: the standard of living of a divorced woman will drop to one-third of what it was within one year after her divorce. A shocking situation! What's worse is that she usually has a couple of children to raise.
   Similarly, the typical widow faces the same statistics when her husband dies prematurely. Within three to five years, both the widow and the divorcee will be forced to remarry after several years of pure financial horror—maybe even hating her husband for the way he left her.
   You can protect your family now with some inexpensive term life insurance to avoid this potential horror. Later on, we can look at an ownership program for investment as well as protection.
   Would either of you please call me now so that we can prevent such a financial disaster?

Sincerely,

This letter makes the interesting assumption that a husband who divorces his wife will harbor worries about the esteem in which she holds him after their divorce. For this reason, he can be motivated to assume some responsibility for her financial future, and thus will feel guilty if he fails to act on this responsibility. The author recommends that the agent take advantage of these emotions by employing such a letter on the grounds that it is both bold and "in good taste." The letter "may be a little gutsy, but selling is a gutsy business."[23]
   Sales managers stress that the value of life insurance will be most

dramatically evident to a potential prospect at the time a death benefit is paid. Surviving spouses may see insurance money as the determinant of whether they can continue at their current standard of living. For this reason, they may be unusually receptive to a proposal that some of the proceeds be invested in new coverage to protect dependents who now rely even more heavily on the surviving breadwinner. Other family members or close friends of the deceased, confronted with this most devastating reminder of their own mortality, may also be much less resistant to a sales presentation than normally would be the case. But, as one agent warns, "this takes balls."

> If you ever deliver a death benefit, your number-one priority is to get the money back. There was one woman who got a $25,000 death settlement benefit. Her husband had died and Carl [the agent's sales manager] took me on the road with him to deliver the benefit. It turned out to be a one hundred-mile drive. Carl liked the sound of this woman's voice. He thought he could get a sale from the 25K, or at least get into her pants. We get down there. We pull up into a trailer park, in a new Caddy! She's fat, ugly, and drunk. He doesn't want to fuck her, but he still tries to make the sale, an annuity, I think. His lesson was: Keep trying! Keep pumping! Naturally, she didn't buy the annuity, or anything else.

The proposal that parents buy life insurance on their children encounters near universal resistance and, if not revulsion, at least considerable hesitation about the propriety of appearing to bet on the life of your progeny in order to profit from their death. However, agents are urged to advance just such proposals, the most propitious occasion being immediately after the death of a child. At this time, parents are still in the throes of grief, their minds confused and clouded by emotions of loss and remorse. This tactic is especially recommended for work among working-class and lower middle class families whose economic circumstances have obliged them to pay for the child's funeral costs on an installment plan, forcing them to relive the emotional trauma of the child's death each time they write a check for the payment of an installment.[24]

For the agent who employs these methods, there is a strong sense in which nothing is sacred. By desacralizing mourners as prospects, the agent desecrates their presumed grief. Emotional distance and other ritual formalities appropriate to mourning are not respected. On the contrary, the skillful agent moves in swiftly and takes maximum advantage of survivors' misfortune and distress. Viewed strategically, occasions of personal tribulation, emotional stress, or moral weakness are valuable prospecting opportunities that should be exploited prudently but unflinchingly. Moreover, the skillful agent will not enter the scene of emotional shock and pain unprepared and speechless in the face of the familiar but perpetually troubling question: What do you say to someone in mourning? Here as elsewhere, the prospect's misfortune is the occasion for a convincing performance by the agent. As in all other confrontations with prospects, the agent masters the grief and personal loss suffered by the bereaved by means of technique. In such a situation, the immediate objective is to sell oneself by convincing prospects of the sincerity of one's expressions of commiseration, a crucial step in reaching the ultimate and much more daunting objective of convincing prospects to reinvest in new policies the monies they have just received as beneficiaries. The social technology for the management of grief envisions three possible scenarios agents may encounter. First, if the agent was actually acquainted with the deceased, the preferred tactic is to make use of the signal advantage of recalling or inventing some pleasant moment the agent shared with the deceased and, ideally, with the family as well. By giving voice to such a shared memory, the agent's attempt to console the prospect will demonstrate that this expression of grief is not a fabrication. Second, if the agent did not actually know the deceased, but is acquainted only with a member of the family, the favored tactic is to recall, if necessary by creative improvisation, personalia about the deceased that the family member may have told the agent and reminisce about this precious experience. Consider, for example, words to the following effect: "I know you will miss going to the theater with her. Maybe you and I can do that together soon in honor of her."[25] Finally, suppose that the agent has the bad luck not to have known the deceased and to be a complete stranger to the family. In that case, it is still possible to consider the admirable qualities of the family member targeted by the agent as a prospect, proceed on the audacious assumption that these qualities are in some way due to the deceased, and share this reflection with the prospect. At that point, a discreet and swift exit is called for, but not without asking the prospect for an early meeting so that the agent can learn more about the deceased. At that time, of course, the question of the prospect's financial security needs will be raised as well.[26]

Training manuals also emphasize the importance of employing friends as potential prospects. The agent's friends are thereby instrumentalized as a means to a commercial end. Novice agents who suffer from misplaced sensitivities about using friends to generate commissions are reassured with lessons in commercial casuistry. Prospecting among friends is said to be an economic imperative in the life insurance business. In order to survive, agents must take advantage of all available sources of prospects. Since friends are quite likely to be helpful in furthering the agent's interests, good business sense dictates that the agent capitalize on this resource. Moreover, it is said to be a mistake to suppose that friends will object to being used in this way. Were the roles reversed, they would do the same themselves. Thus the agent's friends are held to share this conception of friendship as an instrumental value subordinated to the interests of commerce.

Agents are locked in a relentless competition for the patronage of a limited number of prospects. In order to succeed in this competition, they must make use of any marginal factor that might work to their benefit. This is due to the fact that the sales process is also an unsparing selection process that promises survival only to agents who do not shrink from the use of any advantage that gives them some incremental leverage over their competitors. Friends provide one such advantage. Agents who refuse to profit by it can expect to be defeated in the struggle for prospects by less discriminating agents who recruit as prospects not only their own friends, but the friends of the agent as well. Thus the logic of the sales process entails that agents who do not prospect among their friends will not survive. This can be demonstrated by considering two agents, A^1 and A^2, and the following groups of potential prospects: P^1 (friends of A^1) and P^2 (friends of A^2). A^1 has a marginal advantage over A^2 in competing for the business of P^1, and A^2 has a corresponding advantage over A^1 in competing for the business of P^2. Given this situation, suppose that A^1 prospects among his or her friends and A^2 does not. This means that although A^1 retains a competitive edge over A^2 in prospecting P^1, A^2 has no competitive advantages at all. Thus in the contest for prospects, A^2 can be expected to lose to A^1.

In sales training programs, agents also learn that their friends depend upon them for expert advice concerning financial security. It is an axiom of these programs that everyone, including the agent's friends, needs life insurance. Who can be expected to provide the most objective and thorough assessment of a prospect's insurance needs? The agent who knows the prospect intimately and is bound by the ties of friendship to act selflessly in the pursuit of the friend's interests? Or some anonymous agent who lacks this intimate knowledge and is not tied to the prospect by the obligations of friendship? Friends who have some appreciation of their own financial security needs will be confused and perhaps even resentful if the agent fails to approach them. Such a failure suggests that the agent is indifferent to the needs of his or her friends or regards them as unworthy of becoming clients. Friends who are not cognizant of their financial security needs will lack the insurance essential to protect themselves and their families. In addition, an agent's friends will frequently deflect approaches from other agents with the reply that they "have a friend in the business." If this parry is effective in warding off competing agents, the agent who refuses to prospect among friends may leave them uninsured and unprotected.

The training literature leaves no doubts about the "tragic consequences" that can result from the agent's scruples or misplaced sensitiveness on this score. A favorite industry anecdote narrates the reflections of an agent who recalls all the important rites of passage in the life of his friend. He was the best man at his friend's wedding, but did not advise him of his new need for life insurance because he did not want to be regarded as an opportunist who would turn friendship to profit. He was the godfather of his friend's first child, but he never explained how the father could secure the child's education with the appropriate insurance policies. He was a guest at the housewarming to celebrate the friend's new home, but reticence prevented him from bringing up the importance of purchasing insurance to pay off the mortgage in the event of disability or death. And when the friend died in a traffic accident, the agent was the first person his widow called. Although the lesson of the anecdote is unmistakable, the training manual makes sure that the agent does not fail to draw the inevitable conclusion.

> Day after tomorrow I'll be standing beside my friend's grave, and I'll still be trying to rationalize my failure to even talk to him about life insurance. I'll be thinking, too, even more bitterly than I am now, about the staggering price his family paid for my false pride and foolish sensitivity. But most of all, I'll be wondering when the time comes to pay my last respects whether, if he could speak, he would say of me as I do of him, "he was a friend of mine."[27]

In short, inhibitions about prospecting among friends are motivated by false pride and inappropriate sensibilities. They are contrary to the real obligations of friendship, and, perhaps most important, they can produce disastrous consequences for the agent's friends and their families. It follows that the occupational demands of the sales process as well as the ethics of friendship dictate the importance of prospecting among friends. Here as elsewhere, the industry literature holds that the imperatives of the sales process are grounded in both commercial necessity and moral obligation. The lesson for the agent, which training programs never fail to stress, is that good ethics is good business.

The training literature does not consider what obligations, if any, the agent has to a friend who does not prove to be a good prospect. Suppose that although I have a demonstrable need for a significant amount of insurance, I am so improvident that I cannot reasonably be expected to pay for it. Suppose that I have fallen down the ladder of middle class affluence, with the result that I am no longer one of those prospects who will "pay and stay." Is it in the interest of my friend the agent to recruit my business? Or suppose that the agent has developed a more attractive and upscale clientele, so that recruitment of prospects is confined to these more lucrative markets. How, if at all, should such an agent approach the impecunious friend? The logic of the sales process dictates that new agents prospect among their friends because they may have no other viable source of prospects. Without their friends' business, they cannot survive in the industry. However, this same logic requires that agents drop their friends as prospects whenever the principle of competitive advantage indicates the utility of this move. Failure to do so may eliminate the few marginal advantages enjoyed by an agent and thus result in a loss of business to competitors. Under these common-place circumstances, which the training literature prefers not to envision, good ethics is bad business, and agents who place the obligations of friendship above the demands of the sales process can expect the process of economic selection to work against them. The result of this decision will be reflected in an agent's inability to meet sales quotas and, ultimately, in the sales manager's unwillingness to retain an agent who fails to perform up to agency standards.

Thus in cases of conflict, the instrumental rules of the sales process take precedence over the moral obligations of friendship. The training literature presupposes that the agent's special obligations to attend to a friend's financial security needs are consistent with the rules of the sales process. However, it is an underlying and unspoken assumption of this literature that the agent may act on these obligations only as long as this consistency holds. This, of course, means that the obligations of friendship, like all other responsibilities, are not respected as such, nor are they acknowledged as having a morally binding force. All ethical commitments, including the moral claims of friendship, are neutralized by the imperatives of the sales process. Friends are instrumentalized as resources for producing sales. The uses the agent may see fit to make of friends depend on contingent factors determined by the agent's sales requirements and market, not on the absolute demands of moral principles. Put another way, the industry literature recognizes that the agent may have distinctive responsibilities to friends. However, it does not respect these responsibilities as moral obligations. On the contrary, it reconceptualizes them as ethically indifferent instruments of the sales process. Deployment of these instruments is decided by their psychological value in motivating both agent and prospect, as well as by the contribution they make to the most cost-effective use of the agent's prospecting time.

There are other ways that training programs dull the moral sensibilities of agents and forestall ethical reservations about employing friends as prospects. A recommended method is to provide the agent with set "approaches" or scripts that are designed to "break the ice." One agent describes the purpose of such scripts in the following terms.

> You know, you call somebody up. They say: "Who do you work for?" But you're not supposed to let them interfere with your track. So you don't answer. You just keep going. Actually, on the phone tracks it has expressions like "Uh . . ." You're supposed to say: "Uh . . . uh . . ." It keeps the person at the other end from asking any questions. Most important, it keeps the other person from saying "No!" too early.

These scripts serve several functions. Most obviously, the agent is able to take prospects by surprise, disarming them intellectually and depriving them of plausible reasons for refusing to agree to a sales interview. Since the friend does not know that the agent is relying on a script, much less a standardized text that has been used on numerous other occasions, the friend is deceived. The agent does not act openly and honestly, but disingenuously and deceitfully. Moreover, in concentrating on the correct performance of the script—which has been committed to memory and rehearsed in role-playing sessions with the sales manager—agents view their own conduct dramaturgically rather than ethically. They focus on the features of their presentation that make it a successful and convincing performance, not on its moral import. Indeed, even the decision to script an interaction with a friend seems to presuppose a prior choice, or at least an implicit decision, to bracket the ethics of friendship in favor of other more utilitarian considerations. Exclusive concentration on the dramaturgic aspects of the performance in order to sell a sales interview frames the agent's conduct in such a way that it is immunized against ethical self-criticism. The agent is merely playing a role. We do not blame the performer for the crimes of Macbeth. On the contrary, convincing performances of this role are commended, or even acclaimed. Training programs conceive of the performance of agents in the same way. As a result, agents are insulated against troublesome and cost-ineffective ruminations on the relationship between sales quotas and the ethics of friendship, deliberations that would compromise their ability to sell.

A typical prospecting script runs as follows.

Hello, Bill. This is your friend Chuck. Do you have a moment?

I don't know if you've heard that I'm now an agent with Verity Life. I've been looking over the company's products and services, and I've come across some ideas that have been of real interest and value to many people like you.

I don't know whether you'll find they apply to your situation, but it will only take a few minutes for you to find out.

So could I stop over to see you on Thursday at 2:00, or would sometime during an evening be better for you? [Prospect claims he is too busy or has no interest] Bill, I understand how you feel. But it's interesting that people in your position are the very ones who find this service of most value. Since it will take only minutes for you to decide whether this idea might be of value to you, could I stop over to see you on Thursday at 2:00, or would sometime during an evening be better for you?[28]

In employing this approach, the agent solves several problems simultaneously. The script establishes Chuck's credentials by identifying him as a representative of an insurance company. It also leads Bill to believe that he falls into an indefinitely large group of potential clients of this company who may actually require Chuck's services. Thus it is implied that Bill has important and currently unsatisfied financial security needs and, therefore, may be in a financially precarious or even dangerous situation—all the more reason why he should agree to this innocuous interview. Although Chuck puts Bill on notice that he is calling in his capacity as an insurance agent, he does not actually seem to make any attempt to sell Bill anything. On the contrary, Chuck defines the objective of the interview so that it appears to be in Bill's interest, not his own. The question of whether the services Chuck has to offer are really what Bill needs is left to Bill to settle, a tactic that can be expected to eliminate many of the objections Bill might pose to such an interview. By proposing both a specific and an open date for the meeting, Chuck makes it much more difficult, impolite, and potentially embarrassing for Bill to maneuver his way out of the interview. Can Bill spare no time at all, not even a few minutes, to speak with his friend?

Consider an alternative script with an additional advantage.

Hello, Alex? This is Karen. Do you have a moment? I don't know if you've heard that I'm now an agent with Verity Life. In looking over the full financial services we provide, I saw something that might be of interest and value to you.

It's about your auto and homeowner's insurance. If you qualify, Verity Life may be able to offer you a better buy. Before you pay your next premium, I think you should hear how I believe we can give you more protection for your money.

When does your auto policy come up for renewal? And your home-owner's?

[Objection by prospect]

Actually, Alex, I'm not calling to sell you anything at this time. I'd just like to know when your auto and homeowner's policies expire.

About 30 days before then, I'd like to review your coverage with you—to see if Verity Life can offer you a better buy for your premium dollar. If we can't, at least I can give you a better understanding of what you have. When does your (auto/homeowner's) policy come up for renewal?[29]

Here the agent appeals more directly to the concrete self-interest of her friend by identifying specific benefits that may be expected to result from the interview: lower auto or homeowner's insurance rates. Karen's real purpose in proposing the interview, which this script intentionally conceals from Alex, is to use auto and homeowner's insurance premiums as a bridge over which Alex will be moved to a discussion of life insurance, the main source of Karen's income. Here again, the agent employs stealth, trickery, and deceit, placing her friend off-guard and convincing him to agree to a meeting he might well reject if he were aware of the dramaturgic strategy deployed against him, the agent's lack of candor, and the real purpose of the interview.

NAMING NAMES: REFERRED LEADS

It is also essential to employ friends and acquaintances as referrals and sources of referred leads, potential prospects to whom the friend will vouch for the competence and probity of the agent. In the industry, this is the preferred mode of prospecting. It guarantees that the agent sells only to those who "know" the agent, no matter how peripherally or superficially, thereby insuring improved ratios of sales interviews to prospecting hours. Astute agents also make sure that friends generate as much useful informa-tion as possible about referred leads—their domestic and occupational circumstances and their interests and needs. This strategy of turning friend-ship to profit has a dual function. The friend produces referred leads by means of letters of introduction or telephone calls, scripts for which the agent always has at hand. In addition, the friend qualifies the prospects named by supplying information about them, thereby saving the agent considerable time and effort.

When is it appropriate to ask for referrals? Any time the agent is in a position to speak with others about the people they know. An ideal opportunity is the delivery of a claim check or a policy. On such an occasion, agents can reasonably suppose that the potential referee is satisfied with their performance and will be amenable to a request for assistance. However, agents are trained to seek referrals under a remarkable variety of circumstances: when they have completed a presentation, regardless of whether it was successful; when they are making a service call—for example, to renew auto or homeowner's insurance or to answer a client's questions about a policy; when they are patronizing service personnel; and even when they are engaged in otherwise innocuous conversations with friends or acquaintances—in other words, when agents are, at least from the standpoint of their interlocutors, not functioning as sales personnel at all. In sum, the principles governing referrals do not recognize the concept of agent free-time, privacy, or leisure, nor do they acknowledge the specificity of roles, either on the part of agents or of their interlocutors. Regardless of the circumstances of their lives and the social setting in which they find themselves, agents are always on the job, prospecting or pursuing referred leads. Does the interlocutor occupy a privileged place in the life of the agent, a position that is protected by status barriers, hedged in by ritual prohibitions against violations of social distance, or defined by codes that inhibit transgressions against rights or prerogatives? No matter. These considerations cannot stand in the way of the agent, for whom the interlocutor is always either a potential prospect or a potential source of referred leads.

Thus the principles covering referrals require that the agent be shameless and bold, without honor but not without cunning and tact. Naturally, the strategy and tactics of referred leads are matters much too serious to be left to the imagination or ingenuity of agents. Their performance in this area is fully scripted by the sales process, maximizing the chances that an approach to a potential referee will be delivered smoothly and "naturally"—as if it were unforced, uncalculated, and unrehearsed. This appearance of unaffected spontaneity is, of course, achieved only by carefully memorizing the script and role-playing the approach to the referral in rehearsals with the agent's sales manager. Consider the following referred lead track, a typical script drawn from an industry training manual.

Alex, I'd like to ask for your help. I'm interested in meeting people—people who, like you, are responsible, concerned about their future, their family, their business.

I'm sure a person such as yourself knows many other responsible people. That's a fair assumption, isn't it?
[Alex replies]
To help you think of some of these people, let me ask you: Who are your best friends? Who was the last person to receive a promotion in your office? Who recently had a baby? Etc.
[Alex replies]
Well, thank you very much. You've been very helpful. Now I'd like to know a little more about each of these people.
What is Mr. Smith's full name, his address? And phone number? About how old is he? Where does he work?What does he do there? How many children does he have?
What are their ages?
[Alex replies]
I certainly appreciate your taking the time to tell me about these people. When I have the opportunity to talk to them, I'll mention that I know you and that I've recently done some work for you.
I'll be sure to let you know the results of my contacts with these people.[30]

The training manual stresses that each line of the script has been "selected and worded for maximum effectiveness."[31] For example, the phrase "And who else?" should be repeated several times after each category of names produced by the referee—best friends, colleagues or co-workers most recently promoted, and so on. This is designed to produce what the training literature calls a "multiplier effect." Agents are trained to expect that if they repeat "And who else?" with an appropriate air of persistence, friendliness, and expectation, without hesitation and embarrassment and with pen in hand, their chances of wrenching more names from the referee will be increased. They are also taught not to interrupt the referee with questions about the referrals. In order to maintain the flow of names, agents write each name on a separate prospect card, an essential item in their apparatus that they always have at hand. When the referee can no longer recall names in a certain category, agents move the referral process on to the next category. And when this process has finally exhausted the referee's memory bank of acquaintances and has compelled the referee to spin completely through the Rolladex of his or her mind from A to Z, agents return to the referee's first name and begin to extract qualifying information about each referral.

What to do if the referee cannot remember a crucial piece of information, such as the address or phone number of a prospect? Ask the referee to look it up. This tactic has the additional advantage of producing more referred leads by gaining access to the referee's personal phone directory. Success here requires considerable audacity. Consider the referred lead tactic developed by agent Rick Spargo, who attempts to unlock private files by telling his contacts that he wants to be included in their "Personal Directory." When this request produces the question he wants to elicit—"What's that?"—Spargo replies that it is the contact's personal phone book, and then asks the contact to open the file and record his name. This accomplished, Spargo makes his move: "Incidently, there are some other people in that book I'd love to meet."[32] Indeed, more aggressive agents will not ask for referrals, but expect them. After all, in the fact-gathering stage of an interview, agents hear names of many people associated with the prospect. If they only listen carefully for these names, write them down, and then tell the prospect they want permission to get in touch with these people, agents will be rewarded with a list of names longer than they could expect from the more pusillanimous approach of asking, "Who do you know that I can talk to?"[33] An even more daring technique is the "Voucher Method." If the insurance plan proposed by the agent does not require a physical examination, the prospect is asked for three character references. The unstated and false implication is that this is a condition for the acceptance of the policy application by the company's underwriters. If the prospect demurs, the agent drops the matter. However, it seems that most prospects are easily deceived on this score. Believing that this is a requirement essential to qualify for the policy, they agree. As a result, the agent has three new referrals.[34]

In the pursuit of referrals, the agent invites referees to instrumentalize all their relationships—including service relationships based on the principle of functional specificity, acquaintanceships entered into on the basis of reciprocal expectations of privacy and trust, and the most intimate of friendships. Prospecting by referred leads qualifies as a form of interactional espionage. By employing this method, diligent and audacious agents will be able to penetrate files that are presumed to be secure and make a record of their contents. In this way, agents can initiate contact with potential prospects who believe that their identity is safe from scrutiny. By this means, agents can also monitor information generated by potential prospects on occasions when they are least aware that they may be subject to surveillance, and thus perceive no need to exercise care in protecting themselves against security leaks: namely, when they are speaking in confidence with trusted friends or associates.

The advantages of prospecting by the use of referrals are clear. Referrals ease access to prospects. They provide what one training manual calls "one of the best ways to get into new homes."[35] Since the referral leads the potential prospect to believe that the agent has been screened and certified as reliable and competent by the referee, the use of referrals improves the agent's ratio of calls to sales appointments. Referrals are also helpful in enabling agents to focus their prospecting work on the markets they would prefer to target. Ideal entry to a group is provided by its members. Lawyers can be expected to provide the best access to other lawyers, dentists to other dentists, and so on. Prospects who occupy a status that makes them unusually receptive to specific agents and their products can be expected to provide referred leads to friends and acquaintances who also occupy this status. And, as noted above, by proper coaxing and effective questioning, the trained agent can extract from the referee valuable information about the referred lead. Data germane to the potential prospect's financial security needs can increase the cost-effectiveness of the agent's efforts by producing more qualified prospects per hour of prospecting time. Finally, any facts provided by the referee can help agents "personalize" or "customize" their approach. If agents know that the prospect is a new parent or has recently bought a house, this information can help them create a more effective impression in the crucial first interview.

These benefits of referred leads give agents marginal advantages over their competition. They also produce incremental improvements over what their own performance would be without referrals. The essence of prospecting by referred leads is to extract as many potential prospects as possible from one contact. In the approach to each of these prospects, the agent is legitimated by the warrant of the referee's name and the presumed relationship between the referee and the agent. The value of these prospects is also greater to the agent since they have been qualified by means of the information elicited from the referee. In the final analysis, these techniques save agents time, which, as the training manuals emphasize, is their most important resource.

THE COMMERCIALIZATION OF LIFE

In the endless quest for prospects and referred leads, the agent performs a radical reduction in which all the interests and values of life are translated into an idiom of commerce and reconceptualized in commercial terms. In the commercial idiom, the sales process is ultimately driven by commissions on sales. The objective is to maximize sales by improving the ratios of prospecting calls to sales interviews and sales interviews to closes. As the sports metaphors favored in the training literature have it, it's not how you play the game that ultimately counts, but whether you win. The close is the touchdown, the purpose of the game that defines what is meant by success. All the principal criteria for evaluating agent performance—from monthly sales contests to the decision on who wins the trip to Hawaii in January, who gets sent to the big convention to receive a laying on of hands from upper-level management, and who gains a coveted place at the Million Dollar Roundtable—are based on the dollar value of paid premiums. Qualification for membership in the Million Dollar Roundtable in 1988 required $38,000 in first-year commission income. The National Quality Award, which is a prize for persistency in sales, is reserved for agents who maintain in force ninety percent of the business they wrote for at least thirteen months after the sale, thus making sure that the policies they sell stay sold. The less prestigious National Sales Achievement Award requires agents to write fifty to one hundred twenty-five new contracts in a given calendar year.[36] Closing—faster, more often, more decisively, and for larger premiums than your competitors—is the purpose of the sales process.

In the commercial idiom, the logic of interaction is instrumental. Everyone is employed as a tool for maximizing sales. The agent is governed by an instrumental conception of rationality the object of which is to transform everyone, including the agent, into an effective means for the realization of sales objectives that are regarded as ultimate and unquestionable axioms. The instrumental rationality of the commercial idiom is exhibited in various ways. Consider the following history of the closing of a sale reported by one agent.

When I first got into the business, a major client named Jake Feldman needed a very big insurance policy, a million dollars as part of a negotiated deal. My general agent said: "I want Murray Weinberg to fly down to New Orleans with you to close this deal." So Murray and I were on the plane at eight in the morning. He's already drinking, cracking jokes about how we're going to handle this, how we're gonna set up the sale, how we're essentially gonna instill confidence in this guy Jake Feldman. Now the deal was made, actually. So there was no need to do this. But he still felt he had to go through the process. So we get down to New Orleans, we meet Feldman, and Murray, who is a very personable guy, starts to tell jokes. He's got a tremendous sense of humor. Murray's a very funny man, and he's a likable person too. Anyway, he's certainly able to evoke trust in other people. It's the way he handles himself. He's well-dressed. He doesn't look or talk like a typical insurance salesman. When all the lawyers were satisfied and we started to deal with Feldman one-on-one and needed him to sign the application, it was interesting. Jake is essentially a Jewish merchant from New Orleans, a cloaker [New York Yiddishism: someone involved in the selling end of "the rag trade," or the clothing business, usually on a petty scale] in the classical sense of the word. I noticed that when Murray went into action with Jake, he became a kind of a street Jew, if I can use that term. He knew all the Yiddishisms, all the buttons to push. He was able to fall back into his merchant-Jewish, lower middle class, Brighton Beach type of personality. Anyway, Jake signs his name and we say our goodbyes. We get on the airplane. Murray has three or four drinks, and he's a little drunk. It turns out that a couple of things on the application haven't been signed. Murray signs them, using Jake's name. I'm just sitting there laughing, watching all this happen. The bottom line of the whole thing was: Murray even got a piece of my commission. He told me to sign a form, which I did because I trusted him too! And I paid for his first-class air fare!

Consider also the function of the quota system, which requires the agent to produce a certain number of paid policy applications each month. One agent explains its importance in the following terms.

The companies are very concerned about what they call "the comfort zone." Let's take myself as an example: in 1982, making 42K a year, living in a condominium overlooking the ocean near Cape May. They don't want me fishing all summer long just because I know I've got a couple of good cases coming up in September. This is why they have monthly requirements. If you don't make the monthly requirements, you get something in the mail that says: "Look, your major medical is gone. We're not gonna pay for your dental. Your group insurance is gone, but if you want to pay for it yourself you can. And by the way, you no longer qualify for a bonus." This is basically the kind of letter you get. But you're still working for them. It's a kind of incremental ratcheting system they use. In addition, everybody in your agency finds out about this. The general agent lets people know—and he's not subtle about this—that somebody isn't doing well. Usually this letter is late coming to you. So you get the letter on Thursday, and you find out that all this is going to happen on Monday, even though the letter should have come three weeks ago. Of course, if they want to keep you, the general agent goes through the charade of making a call to the home office. You know: "Let me see if I can do something for you." And they always get you a two or three-week delay on these suspensions. But this depends on the delivery of a certain number of apps. Once Chuck [the speaker's general agent] did this to me in a meeting; you know, with everybody in the agency sitting around a table. He goes: "Look, Eddy's numbers are really low. He's gotta get some business in; otherwise he's not gonna get paid." Right in front of everybody. And I almost punched Chuck. I got so angry. Anyway, after you get this letter, the general agent or the sales manager will make the predictable call to some asshole in the home office, and he'll say: "Ok, give him another month to get five apps. He's gotta convert [i.e. deliver checks for first-year premiums] three of the five." And if that doesn't happen, you begin paying your own major medical, your own dental. It's very painful, you know, because you can't live.

Consider also the frequent competitions and contests that companies program for agents, usually scheduled so that shortly after one competition ends, another begins. One agent's view of contests:

One of the ways to generate X amount of business is to have these continual contests. There's also, of course, the annual convention. For the convention, there's usually a bulletin board in the office, or there's an internal corporate newsletter that goes out to everybody—secretaries, anyone can read it. Now on it, you see your status, where you stand with regard to other people and with regard to the big convention. It's all very clear. Also my sales manager was embarrassingly frank about these things. He'd say: "Look, you're not going on convention." At one point, he sent me a letter that said: "No more fun and games! Get out there and work!" Agents who don't follow the company line aren't gonna make it. That's one of the messages they're sending out.

Finally, consider the use made of the agent's wife, a factor motivating higher sales that is built into the agent's domestic life.

One of the ways my general agent would communicate with his agents when we weren't selling enough is that he would address mail to the wife, not to the agent. So my wife would get a letter that would say that I'm not making enough money and that I may not get a paycheck. Or he would address the letter to "Mr. and Mrs." The possibility is that the wife would open the mail and find that her husband isn't performing. In this way, my general agent wanted the wife to pressure her husband to get out there and sell. I'm not sure that's too far away from what goes on in the convention. Here the wife is rewarded for pushing her husband. This is what happens to the good wife, who whines and complains until her husband gets down to business. She has to put up with a fluctuating income. It's a very difficult business in that regard. The cash flow is so unpredictable. The woman is still conceived as the traditional wife, but she's given her due for supporting her husband, as they like to say. They want to recognize the wife for pushing the husband to go out and sell more. You know, it's the trip to Disneyland. The company picks up the expenses for letting the wife do what she wants at the convention.

Thus the commercial idiom cannot accommodate any position inconsistent with the view that human beings are appropriate objects of instrumental control. The principle governing the interaction between agent and prospect is opportunistic. The agent's interest in another person is decided by a cost/benefit calculus for assessing the value that person is likely to have for the agent. This value is established by determining the dollar value of the different phases of the sales process in which the agent interacts with the person, either as the object of a prospecting call, a sales interview, a closing attempt, or a request for a referred lead. The opportunistic principle of interaction brackets all the properties of persons that are irrelevant to their need for financial security. It defines persons exclusively in terms of characteristics that are germane to the purchase of financial security products. Thus the commercial idiom cannot admit any principle that rejects quantitative criteria for assessing persons and their worth. It is inconsistent with any system of values that cannot be reduced to the question: How much?

The quantification of life is an explicit and essential aspect of the agent's work. It is not merely a perspective that the sales process takes on human life, a marketing meta-theory that has no real impact on the agent's conduct of life. On the contrary, it is an operation that agents carry out in their day-to-day activities. Agents perform this operation by representing their interactions with others in purely quantitative terms and reducing these interactions to their dollar value in commissions. The indispensable tool that agents employ in this operation is the "Success Planner": an exhaustive record they compile for each week of sales activity.

At the end of every week of sales activity, agents make some calculations, tallying up the referred leads they have secured, the prospecting calls they have made, the closing interviews they have conducted, the number of sales that all these efforts have actually produced, and the net dollar value of these sales in first-year commissions. From these figures, agents compute the ratios that define performance: the prospecting calls to interviews ratio, or the number of calls required to yield one interview; the closing interviews to sales ratio, or the number of interviews needed to consummate one sale; the prospecting calls to commissions ratio, or the dollar value of each prospecting call; the closing interviews to commissions ratio, or the dollar value of each interview; the referred leads to interviews ratio, or the number of referred leads required to yield one interview; the referred leads to sales ratio, or the number of referred leads needed to generate a single sale; and the referred leads to commissions ratio, or the dollar value of each referred lead. The Success Planner not only represents each person in the agent's social universe as a prospect or a source of prospects. It also reduces these persons and the agent's interactions with them to a dollar value. The calculations entered in the Success Planner make it possible for agents to put an actual cash value on each call they make, each prospect they contact, each interview they conduct, even each conversation they initiate. In this way, agents can determine how much they gain from the contacts that produce business and how much they stand to lose by maintaining unproductive contacts. From the standpoint of the agent, therefore, it is not an exaggeration to claim that "money expresses all qualitative differences of things in terms of 'how much?' Money, with all its colorlessness and indifference, becomes the common denominator of all values; irreparably it hollows out the core of things, their individuality, their specific value, and their incomparability."[37]

The commercial quantification of life is a crucial element in agent training. Training requires supervision, and the effectiveness of supervision depends upon assessment. The performance of agents is evaluated quantitatively, by counting up the prospecting calls they have made, the referred leads they have pursued, the sales interviews they have conducted, and the closes they have consummated. These are, of course, calculations that the agents themselves have made. Since it is necessary for the trainer to know exactly what trainees are doing when they are working independently in the field, probationary agents must be taught to quantify their own performance in precisely these terms. The numbers recorded in the agent's Success Planner are then passed on to the sales manager, who uses them to answer the questions that decide the agent's survival. How well is the agent progressing? What is the quality of the agent's performance in relation to the production of other agents? What are the agent's prospects for achieving the various milestones that mark the career of the successful agent: qualification for the annual convention, the Million Dollar Round Table, and so on? In order to guarantee an accurate assessment of the trainee's performance in all phases of the sales process, the supervisor teaches the trainee to adhere strictly to the definition of each step of the sale. Thus a prospecting call is a conversation in which the agent communicates with a prospect in order to obtain a sales interview. A telephone call answered by the prospect's child or housekeeper does not satisfy this condition. A presentation interrupted by the arrival of unexpected guests who are asked to spend the evening watching Monday night football with the prospect does not qualify as a sales interview, nor does a presentation cut short by the agent's discovery that data from the prospect's absent spouse must be factored into the financial security analysis before a final proposal can be made.

The control of the probationary agent required for successful training depends upon complete and uniform documents—the numbers and numerical ratios that accurately reflect the agent's execution of each step of the sales process. This is why agents must learn to resist the temptation to include spurious transactions in the data they record in their Success Planner. Otherwise uniform definitions of the phases of the sales process, which are necessary for the precise assessment of the agent's performance, will be compromised. The sales manager supervises the trainee's use of the Success Planner for as many weeks as is deemed necessary. Agents are instructed to make entries beginning with the very first call they complete. They are reminded to make entries immediately after each event relevant to the steps of the sales process, thereby insuring that the practice of accurate and complete record-keeping becomes habitual and routine. The sales manager checks these entries regularly to verify that they are entered correctly. The trainee's actual peformance is measured against his or her sales objectives, with a view to detecting and eliminating shortfalls, and ratios are reviewed in order to make sure that the trainee understands the average dollar value of every step of the sales process.

The quantification of life in the sales force is exhibited in various ways. For some agents, it seems to have the status of a moral imperative. One agent comments on the extent to which his colleague Gene was "driven by the numbers."

> We go to this big company that wants somebody to buy key-man insurance. We're on the Turnpike, and Gene, instead of paying attention to the road, is fooling around with a computer. He's calculating how long it will take him to drive from Trenton to Cherry Hill and figures how much his time will cost him if he doesn't make the sale. We get there, and we wait, and wait and wait, even though we had an appointment. You see, Gene wouldn't let me confirm the appointment. He says that in insurance you never confirm appointments because the fucker may cancel on you. Anyway, Gene was one of these guys who kept a computer in his car. He calculated the amount of time the trip took and was unbelievably pissed because of the time he wasted.

However, the quantification of life is a practical imperative for every agent. This is due to the importance of "hitting your numbers"—producing the minimum amount of business required by the general agent—and what happens to agents who "miss their numbers." Consider the predicament of Nick, an agent who, not without considerable justification, describes himself as "a real hustler."

> If you don't keep your numbers up you're out. This can happen faster than you might imagine. Take my company. For three or four years I was in their top forty, one of their top forty salesmen in my product line. All of a sudden, the numbers slip. The numbers slip because I'm doing a lot of brokering, selling a lot of business for other companies. I'm a true capitalist, looking around for my best deal. I get a letter in the mail and it says: "As of September 1, find yourself new major medical coverage. Anyone who pays their premium, you're not getting any more renewals. You have no more life insurance with us." And a litany and a list of things. It's essentially: "Nick who? Goodbye. We have somebody else who's gonna take your place." And the thing is, they're utterly cold-blooded about this. You could be up there thirty years and they'll do this to you. And a guy who's not keeping his numbers up not because he's selling insurance for other companies, but because he can't hack it—he's gone. They'll treat him the same way. You're not makin the numbers, you're out.

Finally, consider the fate of Art Cookman, who actually had been a "heavy hitter" in the business for thirty years.

> Art Cookman was a very successful salesman, a true believer. But he did it by numbers only. When Craig Adams left, the company brought Art in as general agent. Art Cookman spent thirty years in the business, but he didn't make his numbers as a general agent. The agents in his office weren't bringing in enough applications. What happened to Art is something that has always stuck in my mind to this day. He was a typical conservative and a big company man. But, you know, he was treated just like Willy Loman. Fifty-five is retirement, and he was fifty-four years old. At fifty-five, they would have owed him certain things—vested retirement benefits, vested renewals, and other things. Anyway, I walked into the hallway outside his office for a Monday meeting. We were all standing around. In front of his office was a brown box. I don't think he even knew about this beforehand. In that brown box was everything that was in his office. The door to his office was locked and the nameplate was gone. It was fucking over.

Thus there is a sense in which the agent becomes a set of numbers and numerical ratios, confirming, within certain limits, the Marxist thesis that the capitalist work process transforms the worker into an object. If you are what you do, and if agents are defined by their performance, then there is a strong sense in which they are a column of figures, just as, from the standpoint of agents, other persons are the dollar value they represent as prospects or sources of referred leads. Agents, by learning to reduce their activities to the abstract categories of the sales process, participate fully in their own quantification by means of the daily numbers they dutifully record in their Success Planner. As a result, the agent—the actor or subject—is ironically the instrument of his or her own self-objectification.

The objectification of the agent is also a consequence of the fact that the sales process is constituted as a body of texts—training manuals, seminar presentations, lectures, videotapes, sales tracks, financial security plans, policy applications, agents' reports on their own sales activity, and sales managers' evaluations of these reports. This collection of texts defines the social world of personal sales by constituting types of persons—agents, managers, prospects, and referred leads—and the characteristic types of action and interaction in which they engage. As a result of the textualization of the sales process, all of its elements and participants become open to inspection and accessible to the scrutiny of the company. Given the authority that this body of texts exercises over agents and its power to decide their fate, it is hardly surprising that agents see themselves as they are represented in these texts. And as agents see themselves, so do they act, thereby functioning as the authors of their own textualization. Thus do agents become texts or text-analogues, documents that can be written, read, interpreted, assessed, and manipulated in all the ways we handle a text.[38]

Sales training programs do not, of course, characterize the agent's work in these blunt and callous terms. On the contrary, training manuals favor a more self-congratulatory, oblique, and euphemistic language that tends to conceal from agents the truly calculating and manipulative quality of their metier. To the extent that these accounts are successful, agents are deceived concerning the nature of their work. This rhetorical maneuver rests on the assumption that in order to perform effectively, agents must believe in what they are doing. However, such a belief in the legitimacy of their vocation would be compromised, perhaps even destroyed, if agents saw themselves as crass opportunists, attempting to trick and deceive the public and reducing all their human relationships to the cash nexus. If the belief of agents in their own work cannot be sustained in the absence of illusions that conceal the manipulative, opportunistic, and reductive character of the sales process, then it is hardly surprising that the industry literature on sales technique translates the aggressive language of manipulation and opportunism into the relatively inoffensive language of interpersonal psychology.

The instrumentalization of human relationships is celebrated as "versatility": the ability to predict what other people will do, and to act accordingly. The versatile agent makes careful assessments of the intentions and motives of prospects in order to form accurate judgments about their decisions. Versatility also includes the ability to assess the effect one's own conduct will have on others. In light of these assessments, versatile agents vary their interactional style in an appropriate fashion, thereby maximizing adherence to the "platinum rule" of sales: "Do unto others as others would have done unto them."

Regardless of the rhetorical strategies chosen for their representation or obfuscation, the commercial idiom and its conceptualization of the sales process are crucial factors in the socialization of the agent. As one agent puts it: "You live or die by the sales track." He adds:

> The idle chatter of agents is boring in a way. It's all about business. Business, business, business. At the conventions, at bars, even behind closed doors, that's all they talk about. It's: "How did you sell all that insurance? It's tremendous that you sold all that insurance. What was the main market? What techniques did you use?" They like to talk about sales techniques, especially the newest techniques that show up in seminars. But all they do is adapt and refine the system—you know, the sales track everybody learns. They basically live and breathe by this system.

In some cases, the commercial idiom penetrates the lives of agents to the extent that it becomes a social technology for the administration and control of their entire social universe, including their most intimate relationships. Consider the case of Nick, the self-advertised "hustler" we have already met.

> On the way to a business meeting, I picked up a girl who was hitching. We both got high in the car. I pulled off the road, checked into a hotel, and screwed the girl in the hotel room. Now she didn't want to sleep with me right away. I had to talk her into bed. You can pick up anybody if you can sell.

Or consider the marital life of agent Earl Blackman.

> Earl had a sales track for everything, including his relationship with his wife. He divorced his first wife, who turned out to be fooling around. Married a nun so that he would never have to worry about that again. The problem with the nun is that she was frigid. Earl used a variation of a sales track to get her into bed. He was never bothered emotionally about

anything he said. If he could fuck his wife, he knew his sales track was in good shape. Earl was a strange guy, but very bright.

Although the quantification and textualization of agents document and expose them as objects of surveillance and supervision, this process of objectification does not have the consequences that theoreticians of the workplace frequently ascribe to it: the degradation of the value of work, the destruction or deterioration of work skills, and the proletarianization of the worker.[39] On the one hand, it is true that the quantification and textualization of agents make them more accessible and manipulable as objects of managerial discipline and control. On the other hand, it is also true that these same disciplines and controls build into the training of agents varieties of skill and expertise that depend upon the sales process in which they are developed. Trainess become experienced agents, proficient in the techniques of prospecting, interviewing, closing, and servicing clients, and masters of an expertise that brings them an annual income of more than $50,000. These results are achieved only to the extent that agents subject themselves to the rules and strictures of the sale process.[40] In life insurance sales, therefore, objectification cannot be understood as proletarianization. The sales process not only adds to the knowledge and skills of the agent. It also forms a socialization process that develops types and levels of agent competence that would not otherwise be possible. By objectifying themselves in the sales process, trainess constitute themselves as a distinctive kind of human being, defined by the techniques that are a consequence of submission to this process.[41]

3

The Service Idiom

THE FINANCIAL SECURITY PROFESSIONAL

The same training programs that articulate the model of the agent as gamester and tactician of microsocial terrains, mercilessly opportunistic and driven solely by the objective of creating a continuously increasing source of commissions, also emphasize that agents are financial security specialists whose main goal is to provide services for prospects. The sales process is the interaction frame in which these services are rendered. Agents execute, safeguard, and update financial plans. They keep homes and families solvent in the face of disease, disability, and death. They make financial autonomy and a financially secure retirement possible. In short, the agent protects the financial future of the prospect by providing expert advice on how to allocate income in the most profitable and prudent fashion. The benefit for the prospect is self-satisfaction and peace of mind through financial security. The benefit for the prospect's dependents is a more stable financial future. And the benefit for the public is a steady flow of investment capital from the huge policy reserves built up by insurance companies.

Training manuals never fail to stress the correlation between sales, a high rate of consumption, and economic prosperity. In a mass retail economy, we are told, the key to prosperity is progressively higher levels of consumption. But in many product areas, consumers may be apprehensive about the disposition of their limited resources and reluctant to part with hard-earned dollars. In addition, they may lack the wisdom to see that prosperity depends on their willingness to consume. Moreover, a hopelessly complex retail economy that produces an apparent infinity of goods places impossible demands on the consumer's ability to make intelligent purchasing decisions. The sheer number and variety of products outstrip the capacity of consumers to make informed judgments about the relevance of these products to their needs. This is due to a radical imbalance between the number and kinds of goods produced, on the one hand, and the amount of information about these goods that the consumer can gather and process, on the other. Finally, the rapid appearance, proliferation, and disappearance of products threaten the ability of consumers to understand their own needs, which they tend to interpret by reference to the goods produced to satisfy them.[42] In the final analysis, consumers may remain utterly ignorant of their need for certain products. Or, even if they have a dim appreciation of their needs, they may lack the information, expertise, and time to make an intelligent purchasing decision. As a result of reasonable caution and a reluctance to spend their own earnings, and in the face of the apparently unmanageable complexity of the retail market, consumers may elect to buy nothing at all to meet certain needs.

All of these problems are magnified in the case of a product such as life insurance, which is neither a tangible good nor a service the enjoyment of which follows immediately upon purchase. Further, the immense variety of policies produced by the life insurance industry leaves the consumer understandably confused and uncertain. For untutored buyers, the relative merits of different kinds of policies is an arcane mystery that quickly exhausts their patience and interest. Enter the insurance agent, who educates consumers about their urgent need for life insurance, conducts them through the maze of alternative policies and protection programs, assists them in choosing a financial security instrument that will best meet their own particular needs, and leads them to the appropriate purchasing decision. Thus the agent plays an indispensable role in the process that links consumption to prosperity.

The service that agents offer is a plan to protect the prospect's financial security. A favorite industry story designed to motivate prospects employs U.S. Department of Health and Human Services data concerning the economic fate of contemporary Americans who live to the age of sixty-five. Forty-eight percent will have an annual income—inclusive of Social Security payments—below $5,000. Forty-six percent will have an income between $5,000 and $20,000, the average income per couple being about $11,500. Four percent will have an income between $20,000 and $30,000, and only two percent will have an income above $30,000. After the recitation of these statistics, the agent poses the key question: What is responsible for the paradoxical fact that in the world's richest nation, millions of people who have worked for decades to achieve financial peace of mind end their lives in poverty? The answer: "These people didn't plan to fail. They failed to plan." This is the function of the agent: to develop in consultation with the prospect a carefully formulated plan for financial security.

From the standpoint of the theory of the sales process, a successful plan must satisfy several conditions. A good plan is systematic: it takes into account all the factors and variables—from purely personal and idiosyncratic considerations to the economics and demographics of the prospect's household—relevant to the prospect's financial future. It is "personalized" or "customized" in the sense that its objective is to provide the material resources for the realization of the prospect's own needs and objectives. The plan does not attempt to alter or replace the prospect's values. On the contrary, they are treated as the ultimate data of the planning process, regardless of whether the prospect's purpose is to retire at the age of fifty, send the children to medical school, take two vacations a year, or merely survive on a modest income.[43] The plan is flexible in that it can be revised to take into account changes in the prospect's circumstances: new jobs, higher salaries, new family obligations, new homes—all of which are factored into the plan either as opportunities prospects should prudently exploit or as responsibilities, the fulfillment of which depends upon resources they must provide. The plan belongs to the prospect. It is obviously important for the agent to take the time to provide a careful and nontechnical explanation of the plan. However, it is also essential that the prospect participate fully in its formation, naturally under the tutelage of the agent. Thus there is a sense in which it is the prospect's own plan. In the language of the industry, the prospect has bought into the plan. Finally, the plan has a prescriptive and directive force. It is a blueprint for the life of the prospect, an account of the conditions prospects must fulfill and the disciplines to which they must subject themselves in order to achieve the lifetime goals they have identified for the agent. Thus there is a strong sense in which the plan represents the meaning of the prospect's life. It outlines the objectives prospects propose to attain, the means essential to their attainment—the financial benefits that must be produced to realize these objectives—and the conditions that will make all this possible, the framework of policies and other investment instruments that will secure the achievement of these benefits.

What does the financial security planning process require of the agent? In view of the range of variables that must be considered in the plan, the complexity of the planning process, and the diversity of investment vehicles available on the market—some perhaps quite serviceable from the standpoint of the prospect's needs and income, others less useful, still others inappropriate or out of the question—the agent is obviously not engaged merely in taking orders. Life insurance sales is not comparable to clerk-like or over-the-counter selling. In the latter sort of interaction between customer and salesperson, customers enter the interaction with a working knowledge of the relevant products and a grasp of their functions. They may already have made a purchasing decision, in which case the salesperson merely takes an order or transfers goods. This mode of sales does not make the salesperson responsible for understanding the circumstances of the lives of customers that are relevant to the satisfaction of their interests. There is no need to educate buyers, nor is it important to provide them with a judicious presentation of the complexities that must be mastered if they are to make an intelligent purchasing decision. In short, there is no need to frame a plan and convince buyers that, in light of their objectives and circumstances, it is essential that they conform to it.

In life insurance sales, the interaction between customer and salesperson is governed by quite different considerations. Although prospects may have some conception of their financial security needs, their understanding of these needs is generally diffuse and imprecise. Some needs are mutually unsatisfiable. Prospects may not comprehend that it is impossible, for either logical, psychological, or financial reasons, to achieve everything they want or claim to need. Further, they may not have prioritized their needs. This would require decisions about which needs should take precedence and which values should be sacrificed in order to satisfy others. In addition, prospects may not have considered what they must do to fulfill these needs, what steps, means, and instruments are necessary for this purpose. As a result, they may not realize that they lack the resources required to meet their needs. These considerations indicate that prospects do not conceive of the circumstances of their lives from the perspective of financial security. They do not think about their needs from the standpoint of the concepts and logic of financial security and the requirements this standpoint entails. As a result, they have no conception of the discipline to which they must subject themselves in order to meet these needs: the regular increments of saving that provide a rigorous framework in which their lives will be cast for the indefinite future.

It follows that, as the industry likes to claim, selling life insurance must be "creative." The agent works with prospects who may not realize what their needs and wants really amount to, what they imply, or what they require. Above all, they may fail to appreciate their need for the agent's services. In meeting his or her responsibilities to the prospect, so the training manuals claim, the agent functions as a financial security professional. The financial security planning process requires the professionalization of life insurance sales. In a culture that celebrates the professional ideal as the epitome of all impersonal interactions, perhaps it is not surprising that the industry never ceases to remind agents of their status as professionals.

The agent's professionalism and the importance of developing, cultivating, and marketing it are basic premises of the sales process. Consider one agent's observations on the importance of what the industry calls "selling your professionalism."

> My experience has been that managers always push the agent to join professional organizations. Organizations I was told to join were, first, the NALU [National Association of Life Underwriters], both the local and state chapters, and the national organization as well. What you have to do on the local level is to put on community-type programs. If you're a member of the NALU, you put on breakfasts that are supposed to be on financial planning. The company thinks it's important for you to get the community to see you in a professional setting. You get your name in front of people, but in the right context: "Tom Miller, Vice-President of the local NALU will speak on individual financial planning." This gives you a quasi-professional identity. It tells people you're somebody who can be trusted. It gives them the feeling that you're a professional.

In certain respects, the agent is said to resemble the accountant, the attorney, and the physician. Like these other professionals, the agent claims to be an expert in the solution of certain problems in which the public has a substantial interest. The agent places this expertise at the disposal of a client, who receives confidential advice based on an ethic that defines what qualifies as competent service and responsible performance. The objective of agents is not to sell particular policies or financial security instruments, but to apply their knowledge and skills to the long-term financial security problems of the client, thereby establishing a permanent service relationship. This is why training manuals describe the agent as a "financial doctor." The buyer/seller conception of salesmanship is relegated to the pioneer days of personal selling. It is replaced by the professional/client relationship, in which the function of the agent is to assist clients in solving their problems by applying specialized skills and offering expert advice. Selling is thereby reconceptualized as a dialogue between the expert and the client, a relationship based on trust and confidence on the side of the client and competence and confidentiality on the part of the expert.

In what respects does the insurance industry make a claim for the professionalization of the agent's role? What conditions are agents said to satisfy that qualify them as professionals? When training manuals stress the professionalism of agents, what behavior, norms, and criteria are at stake? At the risk of some oversimplification, it can be said that in the life insurance industry, a profession is conceived along three axes: a cognitive dimension, a normative dimension, and a status dimension.

As regards the cognitive dimension, the industry doctrine of the professionalism of agents is grounded in a claim to expert knowledge that requires a formalized period of training. This claim to expertise is the basis of the contention that professionals are competent to solve problems that are important not only to the clients they serve, but also to the public at large: for example, medical problems of personal illness and public health, legal problems of personal injury and the protection of property; and practical economic problems of the protection of income and savings and the achievement of financial security.

As regards the normative dimension, the doctrine of the professionalism of agents is grounded in an ideal of service. The professional receives the trust and patronage of the public. This is said to be based on the principle that professionals will resolve any conflicts between their own interests and those of the client in favor of the latter. This principle of conflict resolution is, in turn, anchored in an ideal of service, which is the basis of the willingness of prospects to trust agents with the management of their financial resources. Indeed, in the life insurance industry, espousal of this ideal seems to be the main criterion employed to differentiate professions from other service occupations. Professionals do not merely perform a service. In addition, their work is undertaken primarily in the interest of the client. They provide a service in order to meet client needs, as opposed to performing the same service merely in order to produce an income.

As regards the status dimension, the distinctive characteristic of professional work is the prestige its practitioners enjoy. In the insurance industry, prestige is chiefly determined by a relatively high income and standard of living. However, it is also a function of special prerogatives such as occupational autonomy. Occupational autonomy is based on the premise that recipients of expert services are not competent to provide these services for themselves, nor do they have the knowledge to evaluate the quality of the services they receive. Under these conditions, who should have the responsibility for exercising surveillance and control over the performance of expert services? The professional's answer is, of course: the experts themselves. This means that the professional controls the producer/consumer relationship. Professionals may be understood as producers who define both what the needs of the consumer are as well as what is required to meet these needs. Thus the professional also decides what activities fall within the practice of the profession. Medicine is basically what physicians say it is. They decide what sorts of conditions qualify as "medical" and what constitutes proper medical treatment. From the standpoint of the life insurance industry, the financial security of a client is essentially what trained agents say it is. They determine whether prospects are "exposed": in other words, whether their income and savings are sufficient to protect them from the economic uncertainties of life. The agent, not the client, is the ultimate authority in deciding what is in the interest of the client. That is because this decision depends upon expertise the client lacks. As a result of the commitment of the agent to the service ideal, the client as well as the public are assured of the benefits of technical competence and professional integrity. In exchange for these benefits, the agent receives trust from the client, respect from the community, relative freedom from lay supervision and interference, and a substantial remuneration for services rendered—all of which, of course, contribute to occupational prestige and the enjoyment of a higher social status.[44]

THE SERVICE IDEAL

The service ideal is clearly the principal basis of the industry's claim on behalf of the professional status of insurance sales. Although industry literature insists upon the expertise of agents as financial security specialists and their knowledge of the "principles of life insurance," these factors are stressed only insofar as they bear upon the ability of agents to measure up to the requirements of the service ideal. And although claims about the important role of agents in the economy and their function as trusted financial advisors are invariably part of the standard rhetoric of industry publications on the value of life insurance sales, there is considerable ambivalence in the industry concerning the prestige of agents and their work. On the one hand, industry executives know that agents want to believe in their prestige. Indeed, this belief is regarded as a condition for their effective performance. This is one of the main functions of industry rhetoric on professionalism: to convince agents that they enjoy—or at least deserve—prestige. On the other hand, industry executives themselves are responsible for commissioning LIMRA research that documents the virtually universal disdain in which the agent is held by the public. The conclusions established by this research only confirm what Woody Allen told us some years ago at the end of *Love and Death*: if you have ever spent an evening with an insurance agent, you know there are some things worse than death itself.

The insurance agent as an object of contempt and loathing is a theme that appears repeatedly in interviews with agents. General terms such as prestige or esteem rarely appear in these conversations. On the contrary, agents reduce the abstract issue of prestige to observations about the concrete details of their work world, the history of their own sales experience, the indignities to which they are subject, and the frustrations they are expected to endure. Two complaints are especially frequent: the hours wasted in waiting for prospects who do not keep appointments, and the indifferent, ill-mannered, or insolent treatment agents receive at the hands of employees near the lower end of organizational charts—gatekeepers whose job is to isolate the prospects from the agent. As regards the former complaint, one agent reports as follows:

> Very rarely do you get to see the person you want to see without waiting a very long time. You know, your time is valuable too. If you're a salesman, it's actually more important than for a lot of other people. Believe me, you read a lot of *Time* magazines.

As regards the latter complaint, the same agent adds:

> Something else that I often notice when I go into an office—a lot of my friends have this, in fact. There is a sign in a lot of these places. You walk in and it says: "Absolutely No Solicitors!" You know, it's the first thing you see. Really, what they're saying is: "No goddamn salesmen, no insurance salesmen, no pharmaceutical salesmen. We don't want any of you jerk-offs here without seeing so-and-so." And so-and-so is the lowest paid, lowest-rung person, who now has a chance to assert his or her authority over you. These are the people you have to deal with, who just can't wait to shit all over you. It's very frustrating.

How do agents carry on in spite of these frustrations? How do they take it? This agent claims there are no satisfactory solutions to this problem.

> How do I take it? You really get shit on in this business. Car salesmen, aluminum siding salesmen, insurance salesmen—you're really garbage. The insurance industry, of course, is aware of this, but they don't want the agent to think of himself that way. For obvious reasons. But, believe me, you're really treated shitily. For me, it's very difficult. I'm not able to wash it off. I'm always going to these office complexes where there are doctors, accountants, and lawyers. You go in there and you start knockin on doors. Sometimes the secretaries will let you in. I'll be sitting there, and there'll be a secretary younger than my daughter, right? Who may or may not have graduated high school. She's painting her finger nails, watching a soap opera on a little tv set. And she treats you like you're lower than an asshole. She'll sit there and let people come in ahead of you. Even if you've made an appointment to see somebody. You're on the

bottom of the barrel, the last guy anybody's gonna see. So you make an eleven o'clock appointment. You get there at eleven o'clock. At eleven-thirty, you finally ask this girl, and she just says: "Well, you'll have to wait. He's very busy." And just ignores you. By a quarter to twelve, you wonder what's going on. And all of a sudden you see the person you're supposed to meet walking out the door. He sees you sitting there, and he goes: "Oh! Oh! I forgot about you! Uh, I have to go to lunch." You know? And he leaves. And you ask yourself: What am I doing here? Why am I in this business? You're just so unimportant to these people.

Industry managers do not assume that agents are so obtuse as to believe what everyone knows to be false. This is why industry claims about the prestige of the agent are often framed in an equivocal and oblique fashion. Prestige is said to be something that agents must earn. It is a value they produce in their work as sales personnel. Depending upon the professional—that is, technically competent and ethically reliable—quality of their performance, they may gain or lose prestige. Thus prestige is not a quality that the public ascribes to the work and social status of the agent. On the contrary, it is ascribed—given the satisfaction of certain conditions—to the person of the agent. Unlike the medical student who acquires instant prestige and the charisma of professionalism simply by becoming an M.D., no one gains prestige merely by virtue of becoming an insurance agent. In fact, given the derision, contempt, and sheer bad manners that must be borne by those who have chosen this occupation, precisely the contrary seems to be the case.[45]

Consider the sales process as an exchange of expertise and trust, the delivery of professional services to clients, who in turn place their financial affairs in the hands of the agent. Is this conception of the service ideal nothing more than an ideology devised by clever and unprincipled marketing gurus to bamboozle the unwitting public and conceal the real manipulative character of sales? This supposition, a commonplace in indictments of the greed and deceitfulness of sales personnel, is mistaken. There are two quite different reasons why the service ideal is essential to the sales process. The first turns on the relation between commitment to this ideal and the ability of the agent to stand up under the psychological stress and metaphysical emptiness of life in personal sales. The second turns on the relation between this commitment and the agent's ability to win the trust of the prospect.

THE PHILOSOPHY OF FINANCIAL SECURITY

The belief of agents in their professionalism is held to be a necessary condition for survival in the industry. Training programs generally recommend that the novice agent contact at least fifty prospects per week. These fifty prospects can be expected to generate no more than fifteen sales interviews, from which no more than five sales can be expected. Prospecting, therefore, requires that agents submit to boring and repetitious routines: seemingly endless telephoning, searching through lists of names, repeating the same sales tracks and scripts day after day, week after week. It also demands that agents live with constant rejection. More often than not—according to the industry, at least ninety percent of the time—agents must deal with prospects who will dismiss or rebuff their most ingenious and carefully framed proposals. Even if it is true, as training programs claim, that each "no" brings the sales process closer to the final "yes," the fact remains that agents spend most of their careers preparing and executing presentations that will be overwhelmingly rejected. How to endure the boredom of mindlessly repetitive work and overcome the anxiety and dejection produced by continual rejection? Only by means of what the industry characterizes as a profound dedication to the meaning of this work and the value of the services it produces. The training manuals insist that high closing ratios and spectacular success in meeting sales quotas are not in themselves sufficient to compensate agents for the indignities they are obliged to suffer. For this purpose, something beyond the promise of more commission dollars, a larger office, or an all-expense-paid trip to some vacation paradise is indispensable. To use the old-fashioned language of the standard training manuals, "a very deep-seated missionary type of commitment to the principles of life insurance is necessary." Agents must have "the religion of life insurance deeply ingrained in their minds and hearts."[46]

Phrases such as "the religion of life insurance" function in two ways. Most obviously and superficially, they are convenient euphemisms, the cliches without which marketing executives and sales consultants would find themselves at a loss for words and thus out of a job. However, their uses are not limited to the rhetorical functions they serve in the ideology of sales. Although life insurance agents and their handlers do not think in these terms, such phrases also express a secular theory of salvation that is grounded in a philosophy. Perhaps it is unnecessary to add that this is not a philosophy produced by academic elites, taught in universities, and deposited in scholarly journals and treatises. It is rather a popular or mass philosophy, a *Weltanschauung* that provides an orientation for the conduct of life as a whole. This *Weltanschauung* holds that the ultimate purpose of life is financial security. It responds to the fear of the middle classes that their struggle to acquire and preserve financial assets will come to naught. The philosophy of financial security addresses the anxieties of prospects whose assets are jeopardized by the unforeseeable contingencies of life: economic fluctuations, unemployment, disease, disability, or premature death. The ultimate premise of this philosophy is perhaps the most banal platitude in the immense catalogue of life insurance cliches: "People don't plan to fail, they fail to plan." According to this doctrine, financial security can be achieved only on the basis of a sound life insurance program. As agents repeatedly admonish their prospects, those who fail to plan are damned to a hell of financial worry, uncertainty, and the threat of privation. However, those who plan the acquisition and protection of their assets by means of life insurance achieve the assured and confident prosperity that qualifies as salvation in this world.[47]

More precisely, it can be said that the philosophy of financial security encounters certain facts of life that are experienced as unintelligible, senseless, and therefore unjustifiable: an unequal distribution of the goods of this world that is independent of merit, and the failure of millions of members of the middle classes to achieve financial security in spite of a lifetime of gainful employment. In coming to terms with these phenomena and justifying the ways of the gods of economic life to man, the philosophy of financial security proceeds from the premise that those blessed with financial success are not satisfied simply by the fact of their good fortune. They also need to know that there is a sense in which they have a right to it. They want to believe that they deserve what they have, especially in comparison with others whose fate is less enviable. Thus they want to believe that there are sufficient and unassailable grounds on which it can be shown that the less fortunate deserve their fate. The difference between the financially elect and the damned is not a matter of chance. On the contrary, there is some basis on which the unequal distribution of goods can be shown to be legitimate. Therefore it could be said that the philosophy of financial security provides a theodicy of good fortune for those who enjoy financial security. It responds to the prospect's need to ascribe meaning and coherence to what would otherwise appear unintelligible and arbitrary, and it justifies what would otherwise appear inequitable and unconscionable.

The philosophy of financial security also provides a theodicy of suffering for the less fortunate, an interpretation of misfortune that explains how those who are without the goods of this world managed to sink so low and why, if this is their condition, they deserve this fate. It elucidates the predicament of the financially distressed, weak, baffled, and insecure. It demonstrates why they have proven unable to meet their needs and achieve their desires, and it identifies the sources of their failure. In the end, it gives them hope for salvation by enunciating a path of redemption from suffering. This path is, of course, the religion of life insurance.

Therefore, the philosophy of financial security can be described as a response to the need for an ethical interpretation of the unequal distribution of goods, fortune, and happiness. The response it offers is a theodicy of fortune and misfortune. The theodicy is voluntaristic: your fate is determined by the decisions you make and the patterns of action that result from them. It is also fully rational: your fate can be exhaustively explained on the basis of these decisions, the circumstances under which they are made, and the consequences that follow from them. Because this theodicy is rational and voluntaristic, in the final analysis there is no discrepancy between destiny and merit, no *hiatus irrationalis* between the way things are and the way they ought to be. Ultimately, you get what you deserve.

It follows that the performance of a sales track may be understood as a promise of salvation in this world addressed to those who stand in need of it: the middle classes who satisfy the conditions that qualify them as prospects. From the standpoint of prospects, the agent provides a cure for the soul by identifying the factors responsible for suffering, specifying how salvation can be achieved, and setting out the steps prospects must take in order to redeem themselves from the Adamic state of financial worry and insecurity. The path to redemption requires that prospects embrace the mission that the agent entrusts to them. They must work out their own salvation under the guidance of the agent. Salvation is guaranteed by an ethical imperative: systematic saving through the purchase of financial security instruments. Prospects impose the requirements of this imperative on themselves by conducting their affairs and disciplining their lives so that, in the language of industry rhetoric, they "pay themselves first." In other words, they scrupulously maintain the regular payments of premiums on their policies, assuring that they remain in force and, coincidentally, also establishing the agent's record for persistency. The prospects' salvation is legitimate because it is their own achievement. Redemption is the product of their own intelligent planning and discipline, practiced under the tutelage of the agent.

The less fortunate are those who reject the mission enunciated by the agent. The prospect as the mindless consumer who lives for the here and now fails to regulate his or her life by placing it at the service of a comprehensive financial security plan. The profligate, the indolent, the negligent fail to act on the ethical imperative of financial planning. By refusing to systematize their values and structure their lives according to the demands of the philosophy of financial security, they fail to plan. This means that they fail in the most important of life's enterprises. Thus they live thoughtlessly, capriciously, incoherently, and irrationally. However, prospects who accept the agent's mission for their lives and buy into a personalized financial plan, assume a task that transcends their immediate consumption interests. By serving the higher values of financial security, they transform themselves, organizing their lives within the framework of the plan and following its dictates.

Thus it can be said that the philosophy of financial security articulates an internally consistent interpretation of the prospect's economic circumstances. It represents a rational stand in the face of the irrationality of the mass retail economy, and a systematic and disciplined position in opposition to the uncertainty and caprice of individual economic existence. As a concept of redemption—emancipation from suffering, distress, uncertainty, the consequences of sickness, and, in a sense, even from death itself—it expresses a conception of the world and a set of values. These values reconceptualize, systematize, and control human conduct by prescribing rules for how to live in view of the kind of world one confronts. In framing and enunciating these ideas and values, agents perform intellectual tasks that are not conventionally asssociated with their work. Indeed, insofar as they are the bearers—the representatives and distributors, even if not the architects—of a certain conception of life and the artificers of techniques about how to market and distribute this conception, it can even be contended that they function as intellectuals.[48]

Insurance agents constitute the priesthood of the religion of life insurance, the ministers and guardians of financial security planning. Because life insurance sales is legitimated as a high calling based on ethical imperatives, conscientious agents do not wait for the financial exigencies of life to bring business their way. For the prospect whose health and security are at stake, tomorrow may be too late. Because of the obligation to safeguard the financial future of clients, it is incumbent on the agent to convince them "to buy what they think they do not need today so that they will have it when they do need it, which quite likely will be when they are unable to get it."[49] This obligation makes it possible for agents to take pride in the fact that they are sales personnel. Agents justify their work by conceiving of it not as a commercial transaction, but as an exercise of moral responsibility. This is one of the reasons why training programs require agents to analyze their own financial security requirements and make the commitment to buy the life insurance necessary to meet them. Only in this way—by acting on the same motives and interests they ascribe to their prospects—are agents able to believe in the sales process they re-enact day after day. Without this belief, these re-enactments lack the conviction and enthusiasm agents need to face their daily quota of boredom and rejection.

THE FORMATION OF TRUST

When agents guarantee their own financial security or purchase generous insurance benefits for their families, they achieve more than self-authentication, a demonstration to themselves that they are committed to the value of financial security and a validation of their belief that a life in sales has some meaning beyond the next close. They also prove their sincerity to the prospect, and thus establish that they are worthy of trust. This is why agents are taught to bring to sales interviews a graph displaying their own insurance portfolio. The prospect can trust only those agents whose own insurance programs demonstrate a consistency between claims and real beliefs, between avowals and actual commitments. As one agent observes:

> Selling your family members is great for the company. It's based on a "Put your money where your mouth is" kind of thinking. They want you to be able to tell a completely blind prospect, someone you don't know: "Look, I own this insurance, my mother owns this insurance, my brother owns this insurance. I wouldn't sell them something to hurt them, so I wouldn't sell you something to hurt you." It's a way of getting the apps in, it's an easy sale, and it's a way of gaining the trust of prospects.

Agents must do for themselves what they propose to do for the prospect. In this regard, agents are instructed in the importance of subjecting themselves to an unsparingly honest experiment in self-scrutiny: In the event of your death, would your family be able to continue the standard of living they enjoy today? Could they maintain their present home? Would your children be able to attend college? "Have you made your own personal commitment to the product and service that you sell?" the training literature asks rhetorically. "If not, will you be able to convince others of their obligations to their families?"[50] This question highlights the second reason why the service ideal is essential to the sales process.

If agents do not act on the imperatives of the service ideal, they will fail.

One of the main tenets of the sales process is that prospects will purchase policies only if they see the agent not as a salesperson marketing a product, but as a professional who can be relied upon to provide expertise. Prospects can be closed only if they conceive of themselves as clients whose interests are respected and cared for by the agent, not as customers who are being sold. As the training literature consistently stresses, the crucial variable in the relationship between client and agent is trust. Trust rests on the expectation that technically competent service will be rendered. Perhaps even more important, it includes the expectation of fiduciary responsibility: the belief that agents will recognize their obligations to the prospect, act on these obligations, and, in case of a conflict of interest, place the prospect's interests above their own.[51] "People want more than just a product or service. They want you to be concerned about their needs; they want you to inspire confidence and trust and to communicate that you are strongly committed to their welfare."[52]

Consider trust as a dyadic relation. In that case, it can be understood as a set of expectations I have concerning your actions. These actions satisfy at least two conditions. They are of some relevance—and may even be vital—to my own choices. And in addition, circumstances are such that I must make these choices without being able to monitor your actions.[53] If I could exercise surveillance over your conduct insofar as it is germane to my own choices, it would not be necessary for me to trust you. Therefore, trust is a function of imperfect information. Under conditions of perfect information, I would have no reason to act on trust. Under conditions of perfect ignorance, either I would not act at all or I would be obliged to act on blind trust. Under conditions of imperfect information, I may—given the conditions just described—decide to act on trust. Thus the less I know, the more trust I need. In order to reach an appreciation of the importance of trust for the predicament of the agent, several points should be considered.

Personal sales is a cooperative venture.[54] This means that it is a joint undertaking for which contributions from both agent and prospect must be forthcoming. It also means that the contribution of the prospect cannot be coerced or otherwise directly controlled by the agent. It follows from these two considerations that agent and prospect depend upon one another, although for different things. The agent is dependent upon the prospect for the premiums from which commissions are drawn. Once the policy application is signed, the agent relies on the prospect to write the all-important check for the initial premium. The prospect is dependent upon the agent for accurate and reliable information, a comprehensive and valid analysis of his or her financial security needs, and honesty and probity—the performance of the fiduciary obligations that are generally held to govern relationships between clients and their expert advisors. Cooperative projects such as personal sales are impossible if the parties are unwilling to place themselves in a dependent position. Thus the ability of an agent to gain the cooperation of prospects in order to make a sale is linked to the willingness of prospects to make themselves dependent on the agent. In principle, agents could solve this problem by confining their sales efforts to prospects to whom they are known, acquaintances who have some confidence in their assessments of a given agent's intentions. On the basis of their personal knowledge of the agent, prospects could feel satisfied that this agent would do his or her part in the cooperative transaction. However, this is usually not a feasible option for the agent. As noted in the previous chapter, prospecting is essential to the agent's success. This means that agents are obliged to recruit as potential clients persons who do not know them well, or perhaps do not know them at all. In any case, the agent must work with prospects who have no reason to believe they can rely on his or her competence and veracity. Thus in securing the cooperation of prospects, the agent must convince them to take a dependent position. The agent can expect to succeed in this enterprise only if the prospect believes the agent will not defect from the cooperative venture by failing to perform the actions on which the prospect depends. This is where the need for trust enters personal sales.

Trust seems to be essential to commercial transactions that are not fully controlled by either the legal constraints of contracts or the economic forces of markets. If there are transactions that slip through the network of these sanctions or are located at their peripheries, then trust is required for their consummation. Such transactions include interactions in which an actor in a cooperative venture incurs risk because of the relative freedom of his or her interlocutors. If the conduct of interlocutors is not determined by the threat of legal or market penalties, they can exit without damage to themselves before meeting the conditions on which the actor is dependent. Because the prevailing sanctions do not guarantee the honesty of interlocutors, trust on the part of the actor is indispensable to the transaction. If everyone were honest, or if the laws of contracts effectively covered all cooperative transactions, or if the penalties of the market were sufficiently comprehensive and severe to prevent dishonesty or noncompliance in such transactions, there would be no need for trust. Thus the risk that is an essential part of the prospect's trust in the agent is a consequence of the underdetermination of the agent's behavior: the freedom of the agent to exit at will, to betray the prospect, and to defect from the interaction without suffering significant penalties. Trust is the prospect's means of coming to terms with the freedom of the agent and the risks this freedom entails for the prospect. The larger the range of realistic choices open to the agent, the more important trust becomes.

As the foregoing remarks indicate, acts of trust necessarily include the possibility of disappointment. As Luhmann notes, this is because "trust is a solution for specific problems of risk."[55] The predicament of the prospect clearly exhibits the relation between trust and risk. In making a commitment that rests on a belief in the trustworthiness of the agent, prospects risk their financial resources. If they refuse to assume the risks entailed by this commitment, they risk the loss of payoffs in financial security that they stand to gain by taking this decision. What is worse, if the agent violates the trust of prospects, there is a sense in which they have themselves to blame. After all, they made the decision to trust the agent. The literature on sales in the life insurance industry stresses that the prospect is acutely aware of these hazards. Thus the dangers this situation poses for the agent are evident. The agent's success depends upon the prospect's decision to assume the risk involved in trusting the agent. It follows that the agent's main task in the area of sales motivation is to convince the prospect to take this risk. The agent attempts to convince the prospect either by minimizing—or, more usually, by denying—the risk itself, or by arguing that in refusing to assume the risk the prospect will lose the benefits to be gained by trusting the agent. While the relations among trust, risk, benefit, and loss pose a serious problem for the agent, they also open up a tempting opportunity. This is because a prospect who can be persuaded to trust the agent can also be persuaded that the advantages of risk outweigh the disadvantages. Such a prospect can be closed without difficulty.

In the sales process, the object of trust is the agent's volitions, dispositions, motivations, and intentions—everything that is, or used to be, collected under the rubric of character. If character is the object of trust, the prospect's decision to trust the agent is linked to the prospect's perception and judgment of the agent's reputation. This is a crucial consideration for the agent, since it means that trust cannot be established instantaneously, in one encounter, interaction, or interview. Excluding the case of blind trust—a possibility that is not consistent with a sales process that rejects charismatic sales virtuosity in favor of the systematic routine of standardized, tried and true sales tracks—it is reasonable to expect that trust can be formed only as a result of repeated interactions between agent and prospect. In considering what can be learned from these interactions, the prospect will reach some conclusion concerning what they add up to as evidence of the agent's character. Two factors make this situation disadvantageous and quite risky for the agent. On the one hand, time is the agent's most valuable resource, which means that an agent cannot afford to devote too much of it to any one prospect. On the other hand, the agent can expect to close prospects only by gaining their trust. But in order to decide whether the agent is trustworthy, the prospect, at least in principle, needs more time with the agent than it is in the agent's interest to make available.

As a result of this practical dilemma, agents are powerfully motivated to develop strategies for inspiring or creating trust, and thus accelerating an otherwise time-consuming process they can ill afford. This is the source of the agent's need to supply evidence of reputation that will document his or her trustworthiness. Testimonies to the agent's reputation, such as those provided in referrals, are designed to abbreviate the normal period of trust formation. However, it is also worth noting that it takes time to develop a reputation, and thus to exhibit evidence of its unimpeachable quality. Considerable caution and foresight are required here. Although a reputation can generally be acquired only gradually and laboriously, it can be destroyed with virtually blinding rapidity—by a single false move, a suspicious maneuver, or an act of apparent dishonesty. As one agent notes: "It's amazing how quickly your credibility can be blown. And sometimes it's not even your fault." He elucidates as follows:

> A few years ago, I spent several weeks cultivating a major prospect, the head of a big computer engineering firm in Eatontown. At that point, I hadn't been in the business very long. So I asked my sales manager Ed Stockman to come down and help with the sale. Ed Stockman was a real machine. A very nice man, but truly a classic salesman. You know, a product of years and years of those programs in sales technique. So we go down to Eatontown to see this big computer executive. This is probably the most embarrassing situation I was ever in. We're in this big board room. This guy was very nice. He had his accountants there. We didn't have to wait long. We sit down. Ed came in. He wasn't dressed properly, you know, for these people. I hate to put it this way, but these were real executives, and Ed came dressed like a . . . Well, his pants were too short, and so, were his socks. There's a role you have to play, and when you're with professionals, you have to dress like a professional. Anyway, he comes in with this big briefcase, and in this briefcase were flipcharts. This stuff is ridiculous. These were very sophisticated people, and at this stage of the game, you don't sell this way. But before anyone can say anything, he has this huge flipchart on the table. He starts telling them why they should buy this insurance. These two accountants really wanted to just get out of the room. Anyway, to make a long story short, they said they didn't want it, because they were completely turned off by

his way of selling. So he puts down this briefcase and he has this other briefcase that he slams on the table. He opens it up, you know, like a vaudevillian. They didn't want the insurance, but he had something else for them. He was talking faster than I ever could, offering them one thing after the other. They start to get up and leave. But he wouldn't let them leave their own office. They were starting to walk out the door, and he just followed them. I was incredibly embarrassed. And this guy, who I had made the appointment with, when I left told me: "I don't want to see you around here any more. Don't ever come back here again." He said to my face that he had never been subjected to anything like this in his life. So there you are. I was finished. Needless to say, I never went back to Eatontown.

The agent's lesson is clear. In his efforts to abbreviate the process in which his reputation is confirmed for the prospect, he runs a considerable risk of damaging it or, as in this case, destroying it altogether.

Finally, the fabrication or appearance of trustworthiness will not do. Just as a real commitment by agents to the ideal of service is essential if they are to justify their work to themselves, so the same commitment is necessary to establish a basis of trust without which the prospect cannot be closed. This is why agents are exhorted to be sincere in all their dealings with prospects and demonstrate their genuine interest in providing service. "If you are insincere, your prospect will sense it."[56] Pretense, theatricalization, role playing, or impression management are out of place here. As the same training program stresses: "You can't fake it. Unless you truly have your prospect's best interests at heart, you will not come across as a trustworthy person."[57]

This is one reason why thorough financial planning is so crucial to the work of an agent. Trust is a product of the interaction between prospect and agent that takes place during the process of planning. The planning process itself is essential to the development of the prospect's trust in the agent. Working out such a plan calls for comprehensive and candid discussions and close cooperation between agent and prospect. In order to create a successful plan, the agent must convince prospects to share their personal ideals and some of the most intimate details of their lives. This experience of sharing binds the prospect to the agent and establishes a relationship based on trust. Once formed, such a relationship is difficult to shake, since it rests on long hours of joint work and the intimacy of details disclosed by the prospect.[58] It is essential for agents to gain access to this privileged data. Without it, the analysis on which their proposals are based cannot even begin. The process by which the agent gains access to these facts ties the prospect to the agent in a highly personal way. Commenting on the confidentiality of this tie, one agent, perhaps with some exaggeration, claims to know everything about her clients. "We know all about their families. We know details about our clients their wives didn't even know. They've entrusted us with family secrets."[59] In this manner, prospects reveal themselves to the agent and give their trust, in exchange for which they expect to receive the benefits of the financial security planning process.

THE ETHIC OF SERVICE

In light of the foregoing considerations, the sales process can be conceived of as a socialization process in which the activity of sales is governed by an ethic of service. Because sales is a client-driven enterprise, the aim of the sales process is to meet the client's needs. From the standpoint of the agent, each step of the sales process—from the initial call to the final signature that seals the close—is geared to the objective of guaranteeing the financial security of the prospect. In this idiom, the logic of interaction is consensual. Agents address the real needs of prospects. They do not fabricate needs, nor do they attempt to persuade prospects to act on interests that are alien to their own conception of life. The sales interview is a conversation, a consultation in which the agent respects the confidential data reported by the prospect and employs these data as the premises of a dialogue concerning the prospect's financial security needs. The close is the conclusion of this dialogue, the product of an exchange in which prospects provide an account of their interests and priorities and the agent provides sensitivity, understanding, and expertise. The principle that governs this consultation is a fiduciary requirement. The agent treats the autonomy of the prospect as the fundamental value that controls the interaction. In a dialogue based on the ethic of service, prospects offer their trust, in exchange for which the agent respects the prospects' conception of their interests as inviolable. This principle is inconsistent with any system of values that compromises the status of prospects as autonomous decision makers. It also entails that the agent must reject as a violation of the prospect's dignity any sales strategy that employs the prospect as a means to a commercial end or an instrument for realizing the agent's own objectives.

4

The Antinomies
of Personal Sales

The definition of the sales process in both a commercial and a service idiom produces a number of antinomies. Because of the conflicts between an interest in commissions and an interest in service, the sales process cannot be both commission-driven and service-driven. An instrumental logic of interaction that treats prospects as tools of a marketing strategy is inconsistent with a logic that conceives of them as co-equal partners in a dialogue. An opportunistic principle of interaction that reduces the prospect to the variables of a cost/benefit calculus is inconsistent with a fiduciary principle that places the prospect's autonomy above all other considerations, including the agent's sales objectives. The agent as service professional does not market a product for sale to a customer, nor does the agent as retailer of policies perform expert services for a client. The agent as professional is committed to a fiduciary ethic that places responsibility to the client above all other desiderata. The agent as retailer violates at his or her peril the commercial ethic of caveat emptor. The agent as professional does not manipulate prospects to maximize commissions. The agent as retailer, driven by monthly quotas, cannot afford to place the interests of the prospect above the interest in paid premiums.[60] Consider also the following contradictions.[61]

SACRALIZATION AND MANIPULATION

On the one hand, the service idiom demands that agents treat the prospect as a quasi-sacred being. Prospects' interests may not be violated, and prospects themselves may not be subjected to humiliations, desecrations, or

69

abasements that compromise their dignity and autonomy. On the other hand, the commercial idiom compels agents to use the prospect in order to maximize sales, which they cannot do without desacralizing the prospect to the status of a customer and profaning the relationship between agent and prospect as a strategic interaction that serves as a means to an end. Put another way, the sine qua non of the sales process is a commercial goal: the maximization of commission dollars through the maximization of sales. However, the sales process also rests on the assumption that agents can achieve this goal only if they subordinate it to moral ends, the requirements of the service ideal. This means that agents are obliged to act on the premise that commercial objectives must serve extra-commercial moral purposes.

The internal contradiction of the sales process at stake here is a result of the fact that the sales techniques dictated by the commercial idiom produce consequences that violate these moral purposes. The prospect is deceived, tricked, moved like a piece in a game, and otherwise manipulated in the interest of achieving sales campaign goals. Consider the concept of "hitting" a prospect.

> Privately—and when I say "privately," I mean after two Jack Daniels at a bar—insurance salesmen can be utterly crass about clients. There are terms like "Hit em!" That's a common term in insurance. "I'm gonna hit him again, I'm gonna hit him again." What he means is, he's gonna pound away at this guy. "I just wanna get this guy, I wanna sell this guy, because I need the money, because I gotta make a payment on my 280ZX." Or: "I wanna buy this boat. I gotta get some money. I'm gonna nail this guy. I'm gonna hit this guy." Over and over and over again.

Or suppose we return to New Orleans and the transaction between super-agent Murray Weinberg and his reluctant prospect Jake Feldman.

> It's now 4:30, and I can see that Murray is getting agitated. He's very upset that we don't have a check yet. This is what he says to me when Jake's out of the room. He goes: "We've gotta get a check, we've gotta get a check." Let me follow up by saying that this is a $69,000 check. Jake, as I later learned, is a very difficult man when it comes to parting with his own money. I don't care whether its sixty-nine cents or $69,000. If it's his, he wants to keep it. Murray saw this at the time, but I didn't. Jake was looking for a way of: (a) not paying the premium, and (b) he was gonna be in our pockets for a piece of the commission. So Jake comes back into the room and says: "Look, we're going to go out and have some dinner." I thought it was great. We'll go down and eat some crayfish and listen to some music. But Murray is now very, very agitated

that we don't have a check. He looks at me and says: "I think we'll have to eat dinner with this schmuck. He's really jerkin us around." So we have dinner with Jake. Murray is very cool, but also friendly. Jake and him are talking, joking, and laughing. But when Jake gets up to go to the bathroom, he's a slab of meat, and we've got to get on the plane to go home. We've gotta get home, and this fat redneck hasn't paid us yet. Murray hates the South, and Jake gives us a historical tour of the French Quarter. Murray was bored to death. He kept looking at me and winking and saying: "We gotta get the check, we gotta get the check. But we gotta put up with this bullshit." Finally, Murray said point blank: "Look, we'll need the check." But the way he did this really misrepresented it. All we needed was ten percent. But Murray said that because of Jake's age, we needed the whole 69K. By the end, Jake truly trusted Murray and gave him a check for the $69,000.

In sum, the sales techniques employed by the agent violate their own presuppositions. Agents are required to conduct themselves in such a way that they transgress requirements that are said to be essential to the successful deployment of these techniques. As a result, the sales process nullifies the conditions for its own possibility and, therefore, defeats itself.

OPPORTUNISM AND PROFESSIONALISM

The opportunistic principle of the commercial idiom annuls any attempt to demonstrate to the prospect that the agent is a professional for whom all things are not permissible. One of the cliches of the commercial idiom is a criterion of truth: "If the prospect says it, it's true." Suppose I am a prospect and claim that I will accept a blueprint for my financial security only if it satisfies specific interests. Suppose I agree that a certain plan will meet these interests and contend that I can muster the resources to pay for the policies required by the plan. This criterion of truth entails that all these claims are true precisely because I, as a prospect, have made them—the insurance industry variant of the doctrine that the customer is always right. According to this criterion, it is true that I can pay for the plan even if I should turn out to be penniless. It is true that this plan will meet my needs even if, in fact, it places them in jeopardy. On the basis of this criterion, what prospects say holds true even if they contradict themselves or insist upon acting on conflicting purposes and desires. From the standpoint of the commercial idiom, this criterion of truth functions as a maxim of opportunism that simplifies the agent's work in important ways. The prospect's proposals may fail to make sense economically or logically; they may conflict with the facts about the policies available to the prospect and their requirements; and they may contradict the expertise of the agent. No matter. By acting on this maxim, the agent is justified in agreeing to anything the prospect proposes.

From the perspective of this maxim, consider Bruno Falvo, described by one agent as "the most ruthless salesman I ever worked with."

> Bruno Falvo was a guy I worked with, the crudest agent I was ever on the road with. He was from Long Branch, New Jersey, an Italian guy. Bruno just saw prospects as numbers. He'd sell them anything. He'd lie, you know. A guy would say: "I've had a heart attack." Bruno would go: "It doesn't make any difference. We can underwrite." He'd get the application signed, get the app in, and get the credit. Bruno didn't care about underwriting. He'd promise you the world as long as you'd sign the app. When we got in the car, all he'd talk about was prostitutes, what prostitutes would do to him. That's what he couldn't wait to go do. He had a lotta prostitutes that he solicited. He treated prostitutes and prospects in pretty much the same way: You get outta them whatever you can. Bruno was a very strange guy, a very crude guy. For him, prospects were just numbers in order to get paychecks.

The maxim of opportunism is obviously inconsistent with the dictates of professional expertise, which require that agents advise the client on the basis of their specialized knowledge. Thus when a conflict arises between professional expertise and lay opinion, it must be resolved in favor of the former, not on the basis of the maxim that whatever the prospect says is true. This maxim makes it impossible for agents to act as financial security professionals, holding themselves responsible for the plan developed for the prospect. Indeed, a professional ethic does not seem possible within an idiom governed by this criterion for truth. If the prospect's claims are always true just because they are made by the prospect, then no rules of a professional ethic can be binding on agents. A professional ethic ties agents to the demands of their expertise and the fiduciary obligations they owe to the prospect. Such an ethic entails that it is legitimate to close a sale only to the extent that these demands and obligations are met. The commercial criterion of truth eliminates these restrictions. Closing a sale depends only on the prospect's perceptions and the agent's ability to control them. The service idiom places moral limits on the performance of the agent that cannot be countenanced by the commercial idiom. Sales personnel who never take no for an answer and manipulate prospects and referrals in order to maximize closing ratios demonstrate that they have no professional conscience. Service experts who are unwilling to "back the hearse up to the door" and refuse to "sell the sizzle and not the steak" show that they do not have the soul of the salesman.[62]

TOUGHNESS AND SENSITIVITY

In the interest of closing sales, agents are expected to endure repeated rejections and suffer veiled, and occasionally even open, attacks on their honesty. They must master their own emotions, which could threaten to explode into a dispute with the prospect that would be virtually certain to terminate the possibility of a sale. And they must absorb repeated rebuffs to their pride and self-respect and learn to live with the knowledge that they are regarded as crass, deceitful, and mendacious. Consider the position of the agent-in-training.

In the beginning, I had to learn how to use the phone—phone solicitation. That's when I had to use these sales tracks. Cold calling, which is a very bad experience. Every Tuesday and Thursday, I had to stay at the office at night. Because what you do is call these people at dinner time. You know how you hate getting calls at dinner time? Well, I was one of these people. They would just hang up on you and treat you like shit all the time. That's the way I felt. This is a problem with being a good insurance agent. The problem is not to feel this way. I assume this is what they were treating me like. But my manager said: "Look, that's your own imagination. Just hit em, one after the other. Just forget about who they are. They're just voices. And you'll get one outta ten. Don't personalize it. Don't become emotional about any of these things." But it was very tough.

Or consider the everyday degradation ceremonies to which an agent is subjected.

My partner and I went to see an officer of some big company near Philly. This guy was extremely impolite. In fact, he treated us like shit. He said he was interested in an estate plan. The thing is, we saw this guy three times. Each time was more embarrassing than the last. It became clear in the end that this guy was only using us for information, picking our brains with regard to different kinds of proposals we had. He probably had an in-house person to take care of this and just wanted to check up on him. I guess the key here is that as a trainee, I was introduced to this idea that you can't be concerned with being embarrassed or treated like shit.

In order to survive in the trenches where the dirty war for the commit-ment of prospects is fought, agents must steel themselves to withstand these psychological ravages: the constant stress, the attacks on their integrity and their metier, and the routine experience of conflict, fear, and uncertainty. Agents have responded to these circumstances by developing an ethic of cynical toughness. Although the mindless bravado of the Kennedy White House—"When the going gets tough, the tough get going"—is favored among established agents, the ethic at stake here seems to approximate much more closely a pathos of masculine anti-heroism: being able to take it, having the endurance to stand up under indignities, degradations, even catastrophes that have been prepared for the agent by the fates that govern the world of personal sales. In view of the demands of the commercial idiom, it is difficult to see how agents could tolerate the rigors of everyday life in the industry without developing protective insensitivities and a defiant pride in their ability to keep going, regardless of the humiliations they face. The agent who is respected by his fellows—and it is clearly a male agent that this ethic envisions—is precisely someone who "can take it," who can hold his professional posture intact and maintain an appearance of insouciance and savoir faire in spite of the shocks he must absorb.

Agents frequently express the sort of fortitude they respect by using a crude metaphor of defecation and consumption, the prospect doing the former, the agent the latter. The seasoned agent is said to be capable of "eating" immense quantities of "shit." Such an agent, who has endured weeks or months of failure, rejection, and humiliation at the hands of prospects, is said to be able to respond to this treatment with the defiant provocation "Shit on me again!"—a strangely perverse expression of hau-teur and insolence in the face of adversity. This is not primarily a way of contending that the agent can retain his self-respect and dignity in spite of the abominations that are heaped upon him. It is rather a coarse reaffirma-tion of his determination to keep going, regardless of what he must suffer, until he closes the sale. Thus it is not surprising that such an agent is sometimes characterized as "a machine" or "an iron man," which in this context are terms of admiration and respect. If the agent has no feelings, he cannot be emotionally touched or damaged, even though he may be a receptacle of everyday moral and psychological defecation.

On the other hand, the service idiom requires that the agent develop highly refined sensitivities that virtually border on the abnormal. Agents must be attuned to the prospect's needs, wants, and interests. They must scrutinize the prospect carefully to determine how he or she conceives the financial security planning process. Perhaps even more important, they must develop an acute sense of how they are perceived by the prospect, and cultivate their capacities for psychological judgment in order to weigh the effect their own manner and personality produce on the prospect. If the strategies employed by agents to control the interaction with the prospect seem to jeopardize the sale, they are expected to examine their own conduct and the battery of impression management techniques they employ. By means of a ruthless exercise in self-scrutiny, they should attempt to alter the impressions they make on the prospect. The purpose of all this emotional work is, of course, to continually reassure the prospect, to be—and not merely appear—friendly, warm, concerned, and caring; and not just occasionally and in relation to particular favored prospects, but every day and in relation to all legitimate prospects.[63] In short, the requirement of sensitivity charges agents to be honestly concerned about the interests of all prospects, who may insult or humiliate them even as they undertake these superhuman efforts in the direction of moral and emotional refinement.

The demands of toughness and sensitivity pose a psychological paradox. How is it possible for agents to develop the hardened sensibilities and iron-clad defenses of the trench fighter at the same time that they cultivate the emotional virtuosity of the courtier? One mentality excludes the other. This paradox is a consequence of the moral and psychological imperatives of the two idioms of the sales process, which produce two radically different types of human being.

SINCERITY AND DISSIMULATION

Professional sales personnel have an obligation to see to it that their clients treat their joint relationship in a purely professional fashion. For professionals such as physicians, this requirement is institutionally satisfied, as a result of which they need make no special or personal efforts in this direction. For the agent, matters are not so simple. In the insurance industry, the social mechanisms necessary to establish and legitimize professional status—institutions comparable to post-graduate, degree-granting faculties associated with major universities and organizations with the tradition, power, and prestige of the American Medical Association and the American Bar Association—are not in place. This is why training manuals instruct agents—inelegantly, bluntly, and with brutal candor—that it is crucial for them to "sell the prospect on their professionalism." Why should this be necessary? In important respects and for a number of evident reasons, life insurance agents are not acknowledged professionals at all.

From the standpoint of the cognitive dimension of professionalism, agents receive no training comparable to the education of the physician, the attorney, or even the dentist or the accountant. From the standpoint of the status dimension, as noted above, the agent is notably lacking in prestige. Finally, from the standpoint of the normative dimension, the conduct of the agent is not subject to a guild ethic enforced by gatekeeper organizations. Agents who commit moral or legal lapses in their work at one company have no difficulty—assuming that they have established a record of high performance in "making their numbers"—moving to another company, or even transferring to another agency within the same organization. Consider the following account of the arrangements made to retain rogue agents.

> A common practice is that an agent will mail an application to someone in Philadelphia, even though he's only licensed in New Jersey. He'll tell the guy: "Fill it out, sign it, and mail it back to me in Jersey. I'll witness it in Jersey and sign it in Jersey, where I'm licensed." This was the big wink. Everyone was doing it. If you get caught doing something that's really hideous or really embarrassing to the company, they'll fire you outright, ostensibly for "breaking regulations." Otherwise, it doesn't happen. There was one guy who left Covenant Life to work for Verity who was supposedly keeping premiums instead of sending them up to the company. Can you imagine that? Now you're entering the grounds of fraud, felony, you know, stealing. Verity supposedly let him go. But I later found out that they basically suspended him for ninety days and let him do business. At my agency, there is somebody who committed outright criminal fraud. I won't go into the details, because I don't want to see them in print in any form. Anyway, he's still working there. No problem. They licensed somebody else to sign all his applications. Of course the reason is the numbers. This guy is a great salesman, and they wanted to keep him. They worked something out. This happens a lot. A first-rate agent doesn't truly get fired from an insurance company unless he's going to jail. Or unless he becomes a total embarrassment. We might close this little vignette by saying that if you're a really successful agent, it's almost impossible to get fired. Arrangements get made.

Another agent offers the following remarks on the kinds of arrangements that are made in such cases.

> Here's a possible scenario. This is the way the insurance company might work it. I come to general agent Joe Blow and say: "Look, I can supply you with one $30,000 premium every June. But my past record is a little spotty. I went bankrupt. I embezzled money from my previous employer. I did three months in Allenwood" [minimum security federal

penitentiary in Pennsylvania]. You know, I'm not gonna get a license! Let's be honest about this. All the general agents I've ever worked with would say: "Fine. Call the prospect up every June. Call me up, and we'll go see the prospect together. We'll take the application, and I'll sign it. We'll take the case, and when the commission comes to me, there are various ways we can cut you in. Straight cash. Or we make you a consultant of some sort and pay you a finder's fee." All above board and legitimate. In other words, there are ways these things get worked out if I, an ex-con, have business to bring into the agency.

In sum, the life insurance industry expects agents to appear to be what they are not: namely, professionals. This means that agents must endeavor to act as if they were professionals and prove their professionalism to the prospect. They must say what they know to be false, behave in a way that the prospect is led to believe what is false, and suggest, imply, or intimate— whether by means of gesture, impression, bearing, or insinuation—what is not true. In other words, agents must act insincerely. It follows that they are obliged to act in ways that encourage mistrust, for sincerity, as the training manuals insist, is a requirement of trust. On this point, the training manuals seem to be correct. It is essential to trust that anyone who signifies or implies that he or she has certain characteristics should in fact have them. Trust depends upon sincerity in the sense that actors should be what they claim to be. It is their obligation to see to it that appearance corresponds to reality and that what they express conforms to what they are. Without this basis in sincerity, trust would be impossible. But this is precisely what agents cannot do, since it would compromise their attempt to prove their professionalism to the prospect. Because of their questionable status as professionals, agents cannot afford to be sincere. On the contrary, the circumstances of their work dictate a posture of prevarication, in which agents evade the truth about themselves; or perhaps dissimulation, in which they conceal their motives by pretending to be what they are not. In consequence, the sales process requires of the agent both sincerity, without which trust is impossible since the prospect will not trust a demonstrably insincere agent, and dissimulation, which destroys the sincerity that is essential to trust.

THE PARADOX OF SINCERITY

The sales process demands of agents the appearance of professionalism in order to achieve trustworthiness. This expectation is imposed on a service industry role in which the demonstration of professionalism and trustworthiness is not otherwise guaranteed by criteria that agents can satisfy or desiderata that are at their disposal and under their control. The M.D. degree and its legitimation by traditional institutional power and prestige certify the professional status and trustworthiness of the physician, even though an individual physician may not in fact be a particularly reliable person. It is not necessary for doctors to seem professional. They need only be professional by satisfying the requisite criteria. This does not hold true for insurance agents. Even if they are professionally trustworthy, this is not sufficient to prove their trustworthiness in the eyes of the prospect, nor does it demonstrate their professional status. They must also sell the prospect on their professionalism, managing their conduct in such a way that the prospect reaches the desired conclusion about their trustworthiness—which in this case happens to be true.

As a result, the sincerity of agents about their trustworthiness creates a paradox. It depends upon behavior that casts this very sincerity in doubt: the management of impressions undertaken to convince the prospect to believe in the agent's trustworthiness. If sincerity is a natural and unforced conformity between avowals and actions, then it does not make sense to try to be sincere or to devise strategies for becoming more sincere, both of which require the deliberate attempt to achieve a state that cannot be brought about by calculation. Consider agents who are sincere in their attempt to become worthy of the prospect's trust. Their self-consciousness—their knowledge of the circumstances of their role and the conditions required for its performance—rules out the possibility of sincerity. Sincerity produces insincerity.[64]

This paradox is the result of a demonstration the object of which is to establish the possession of certain qualities: the intentionality of the demonstration is related to its object in such a way that the former nullifies the latter. If the desired state of sincerity depends on an absence of intentionality, calculation, or striving, then any attempt to achieve sincerity by intentional effort or deliberation is self-defeating. This is because any such attempt renders impossible the result it proposes to establish. The problem at issue concerns the conditions under which professionalism can be proven. Is it established institutionally, or is it demonstrated by means of efforts undertaken by the claimant to a professional status? In the latter case, impression management is essential. To manage impressions is to create a performance, to produce a show, and thus to dramatize one's attributes or conduct. These efforts depend upon the distinction between the agent and the character he or she represents. They presuppose that agents see themselves both as performers and as the characters that are the product of the performance. By dramatizing their conduct and employing dramaturgic criteria in order to assess their performance, agents make sure that they know they are not what they seem to be. The logic of the dramaturgic situation guarantees that agents self-consciously represent themselves as what they are not, thereby demonstrating their own insincerity.[65]

THE PARADOX OF TRUST

The sales process holds that a sale is possible only if the prospect trusts the agent. Prospects will buy only from agents whom they see as trustworthy professionals who place prospects' interests above their own. In the relationship between agent and prospect, prospects allocate trust insofar as they find the claims and conduct of the agent credible and reliable. Trust reduces the complexity that prospects perceive in the sales process. If prospects find the agent trustworthy, they will not be inclined to harbor suspicions or raise doubts about whether the agent really is the professional expert he or she claims to be. They will not question whether a specific policy is recommended because it best serves their own needs or because it maximizes the agent's commission dollars. They will not consider whether each step of the agent's presentation is an attempt to trick them into a decision that is not in their best interests or an honest attempt to formulate a coherent financial security plan tailored to their own circumstances. Trust also reduces the number of variables in the sales process that the agent must take into account. Agents who enjoy the trust of the prospect are not burdened by the social technology required to sell themselves. Instead of concentrating on the many factors relevant to impression management and the various strategies by means of which they might gain the confidence and win the respect of the prospect, they can explore the prospect's needs and frame plans designed to meet them. Therefore, if agents can rely on the assumption that prospects trust them, certain advantages to agents are clearly forthcoming. Moreover, if the prospect's belief in the agent's reliability is justified, trust seems to work in the interest of the prospect as well.

Although trust limits the range of variables agents must juggle in the sales process and simplifies their task in moving the prospect to the close, it also places certain limits on the freedom of agents to select strategies and tactics. Trustworthy agents cannot act in ways that call their reliability into question, nor can they afford to engage in behavior that would cause the prospect to entertain suspicions about their credibility. Agents must make sure that the claims they make suggest no contradictions, real or apparent.

They cannot take risks that cast doubt on what they have told the prospect about themselves and their work. In short, they cannot afford any lapses in performance that destroy the conformity between avowals and behavior. This is because trust depends not only on familiarity: the confidence of prospects that they know what to expect in dealing with the agent. It depends on consistency as well: the belief on the part of prospects that agents do not make conflicting claims; that what agents say about themselves corresponds to what they do; and that—in some sense that inspires confidence in the prospect—an agent's actions are all of a piece. Consistency requires that one claim or action not defeat another. On the contrary, allegations and actions must be mutually supporting in such a way that they enhance a belief in the agent's veracity and reliability.

If trust depends upon consistency, two consequences follow. The prospect must believe that the professional identity claimed by the agent is consistent with the agent's conduct; and the management of the sales process by the agent must demonstrate this consistency to the prospect. However, the sales process also requires that agents be radical opportunists. They must exploit every advantage and control every variable in the interaction with the prospect in order to maximize the chances of closing. This strategy defeats trust by destroying the conditions under which it is possible. The principle of opportunism keeps the prospect off-guard. Because opportunistic agents gear their tactics to the psychodynamic contingencies of the situation, the prospect hardly knows what to expect next. Indeed, in the ideal sales interview, this is necessarily the case since the interaction is governed by an instrumental logic in which the agent controls the prospect. As a result, opportunism increases the complexity of the sales process for the prospect by increasing the uncertainty of its outcome. Uncertainty also increases the prospect's perception of risk, and thus encourages mistrust. In consequence, the opportunistic agent betrays trust and teaches mistrust, thereby nullifying the psychological and moral conditions under which the sale can be consummated.[66]

The instrumentalization of life entailed by the exigencies of personal sales requires that agents hone their skills, manage their time, and mold their relationships in order to become pliable instruments of the sales process. Agents must do whatever is required, suffer and commit all manner of indignities, and perform whatever violations of taste and principle are necessary in order to close the sale. This, of course, means that the agent cannot be trusted, for a person who regards all things as allowable is unpredictable and thus unreliable. In sum, the sales process, which requires the agent to conceive of all persons and employ all relationships as sources of potential prospects, is inconsistent with the possibility of trust. Since trust is the relationship that agents are trained to exploit most aggressively, it also follows that the sales process is ironically self-defeating. On the one hand, it requires agents to develop relations of trust as sources of prospects. On the other hand, in putting to use those who trust them, agents jeopardize the very relationships they attempt to exploit, thereby compromising their most important source of prospects.[67]

5

The Intellectualization
of Personal Sales

THE ANTINOMIES OF PERSONAL SALES AND THE WORK
WORLD OF THE AGENT

Antinomies are generally identified with a view to showing that they are only apparent. Following the account of the conflict between principles, one expects an intellectually satisfying analysis of the circumstances under which it can be resolved or dissolved. These expectations will be disappointed here. The above antinomies are not merely extraneous aspects of personal sales. On the contrary, they are intrinsic properties of the sales process itself and thus cannot be eliminated. The commercial idiom and the service idiom generate conflicting interpretations of personal sales. These interpretations produce mutually inconsistent conceptions of the salesperson; they conceive of the activity of sales in two quite different ways; and they impose mutually unsatisfiable expectations and obligations on sales personnel. In the life insurance industry, it is the fate of agents to realize in their work the paradoxes entailed by these two idioms and to live through the conflicts they create. The sales divisions of life insurance companies fully document the activity of the agent by reducing it to its various performances, their successes, shortcomings, and failures, all of which are fully quantified and open to inspection. As a result, these conflicts are potentially transparent to everyone, including, of course, to the agents themselves.

But do agents perceive these conflicts? And if so, are they understood as contradictions that cannot be resolved because they are immanent consequences of the sales process? It is the work world of the agent that manifests the conflicts between the commercial idiom and the service idiom. Does this mean that agents also regard the sales process as paradoxical and grasp the impact of these paradoxes on their work? From the fact that the conflicts between the two idioms are potentially transparent, does it follow that agents actually see them?

What are the possible positions that agents can take with regard to these contradictions? Given irresolvable conflicts between the two idioms, how can they be construed by agents? What possible constructions can be placed on the above antinomies by anyone who can be expected to function as an effective salesperson?

In his lecture on "Science as a Vocation," Max Weber argued that the human personality is forged by conflicts between ultimate values, which he characterized in the unforgettable metaphor of a pantheon of gods and demons locked in an implacable struggle for the human soul. The person creates and demonstrates his own humanity by making the hard choices between these values, by deciding unequivocally, as Weber put it, "which is God for him and which is the devil."[68] The values of commerce and professional service are among the possible ultimate positions that can decide the basic orientation and direction of human life. However, the fundamental irreconcilability of these values entails that the struggle between them can never be brought to a final conclusion. This is why Weber claims that it is necessary to take a definitive stand and make a decision, as a result of which the person "finds and obeys the demon who holds the fibers of his very life."[69] For the life insurance agent, this heroic posture is neither necessary nor even possible. Because the work of the agent is itself formed by conflicting principles and values, agents cannot make the hard choices demanded by intellectual integrity and moral purity, the final decisions that produce ultimate clarity about the meaning of life.

Perhaps the humanity of the agent is exhibited in a quite different way, beautifully articulated by another chronicler of the moral tensions of modern life. F. Scott Fitzgerald's understanding of the ethical irrationality of life included the possibility of consummating an intellectually insupportable but morally tolerable commitment to mutually inconsistent principles, a position that exhibits its own kind of integrity precisely because it rests on a self-conscious embrace of irresolvable conflicts. "The test of a first-rate intelligence," according to Fitzgerald, "is the ability to hold two opposed ideas in the mind at the same time, and still retain the ability to function."[70] Fitzgerald's thesis is intellectually more pessimistic and ethically more demanding that Weber's. Perhaps it is also more exactly tuned to the actual meaning of the conflicts between ultimate values and the way these conflicts shape occupational life. However, this stand is not open to the agent either. It would be ludicrous to suppose that agents could remain productive and meet their quotas if they perceived their careers as riven by irresolvable contradictions. It would be equally ridiculous to suggest that consultants could succeed in marketing a theory of the sales process that is recognized as paradoxical, and no less foolish to suppose that marketing and sales executives would assume the responsibility for implementing such a theory.

Strategically and theoretically, the sales process can be effective only to the extent that it provides some means of diminishing the force of the conflicts it generates. Motivationally and practically, this means that personal sales as a career is possible only if sales personnel are not hammered by self-doubt and paralyzed by the impact of contradictions concerning the meaning of their work. The proven successes of training programs in personal sales and the institutionalization of personal sales as a career presuppose standard procedures by means of which the antinomies of the sales process can be explained, obscured, denied, forestalled, or therapeutically accommodated, even if they cannot be eliminated. The same theory of the sales process that creates these antinomies must also immunize the salesperson against the doubts and stresses they produce. It follows that there must be some sense in which the paradoxes of the sales process remain concealed from the agents in whose lives they are exhibited, a possibility which itself seems to border on the paradoxical. As a result, agents would be shielded from the tensions and pressures these paradoxes could be expected to create.

In the ensuing, I outline several different considerations that show why the productivity of sales personnel is not jeopardized by the antinomies of the sales process. These considerations provide a framework for the analysis of an interesting type of case, in which the theoretical incoherence of a practice does not compromise its real efficacy—yet another example of what, following Max Weber, we have learned to call the conflict between formal and substantive rationality.

UNTRUTH AS A CONDITION FOR LIFE

Consider the practice of personal sales from the standpoint of sales personnel themselves. From the perspective of the performers, how is their performance related to the practice and what it produces? How are life insurance agents linked to the execution of the sales process and the antinomies it generates? Agents are expected to perform the sales process correctly: to hone their prospecting methods and sharpen their interviewing techniques and closing skills so that they will be able to meet their regular quotas. The fate of insurance agents, their ability to prevail in a highly competitive industry where attrition rates still approximate a devastating eighty-five percent, depends upon their ability to get all this right. They do not reflect on the possibility that the practice of personal sales, the performances that constitute it, the discipline required by the sales process, the assumptions that they as agents are obliged to make, and the consequences they must accept all rest on fundamental contradictions. Does this mean that agents suffer from a lack of objectivity and a deficiency in self-consciousness? What would a more enlightened and self-critical attitude toward their work achieve? Suppose that agents had a more sophisticated grasp of their work. Suppose they understood the principles on which personal sales is based and the conflicts between the commercial idiom and the service idiom that these principles entail. What would enlightenment amount to in this context? What ends and interests would it serve?

We find a general answer to these questions in a famous observation Nietzsche makes in *The Will to Power*.

> It is not enough that you understand in what ignorance man and beast live; you must also have and acquire the *will* to ignorance; you need to grasp that without this kind of ignorance life itself would be impossible, that it is a condition under which alone the living thing can preserve itself and prosper; a great, firm dome of ignorance must encompass you.[71]

On this view, a certain kind of ignorance is essential to a practice. Ignorance is tied to the practice by the strongest possible link: the former is a condition for the possibility of the latter. Without the ignorance in question, the practice could not exist. Therefore, it could be said that a certain blindness is a condition for the possibility of a certain way of seeing and the perspective that defines it. In fact, agents assure the prospect that his or her financial security is their primary responsibility. At the same time, agents assure the sales manager, who is pressing them for higher rates of sales, that their primary obligation is to meet the manager's quotas. In fact, agents lead the prospect to believe that the latter's interests come first in their relationship. At the same time, they use prospects as tools to meet monthly quotas. In fact, agents attempt to develop their capacities for sincerity, thereby winning the prospect's trust. At the same time, they act on strategies that rule out the possibility of sincerity and trust. How are these facts possible? Only on the assumption that agents do not recognize them as facts, only if they refuse to acknowledge them as what they are: instances of the conflict between the commercial idiom and the service idiom.

Agents can be expected to professionalize their presentations and effectively represent themselves as professionals only if they fail to grasp the conflicts between the demands of the commercial idiom and the requirements of professionalism. They can reasonably attempt to gain the trust of the prospect only if they do not see that the opportunism required by the commercial idiom compromises the conditions under which trust is possible. They can be expected to polish the various techniques for the manipulation of the prospect only to the extent that they do not comprehend the damage these techniques inflict upon their attempt to win the prospect's confidence by representing themselves as credible advisors. The will to ignorance is not a decision sales personnel take to dismiss particular matters from the sphere of their competence. Such a decision would presuppose cognizance of the conflicts that jeopardize the efficacy of the sales process. On the contrary, the will to ignorance is a decision not to know something: that in acquiring and practicing the skills essential to personal sales, the salesperson not only remains ignorant of other things, but also fails to know what these other things are. In the final analysis, this amounts to a decision not to be self-conscious, a decision to limit reflection to a certain sphere of occupational functions in a way that excludes recognition of the conflicts of the sales process. As a result, the experience of these conflicts remains below the salesperson's cognitive horizon. Thus in learning the practice of the sales process, the salesperson also learns the means of rendering the antinomies of this process invisible.

It follows that there is a sense in which the will to ignorance is also a will to knowledge. In order to develop their competence as sales personnel, agents need to know how to ignore the kind of knowledge that compromises their own effectiveness and endangers the viability of the practice of personal sales. This means that they need to know how to ignore the antinomies of the sales process. In short, we can know or master certain things only insofar as we remain ignorant of others. The acquisition of the skills needed to become an agent rests on certain illusions. The illusion most indispensable to agents is·their belief in the coherence of the sales process itself and the consistency between the two idioms that define their occupational identity and make their work possible.[72]

THE SALES PROCESS IN THEORY AND PRACTICE

It may be the case that logically or conceptually—from a perspective that is interested in consistency solely for its own sake and as an end in itself—the two idioms that define the sales process lead to paradoxes. However, agents who actually employ the sales process and sales managers who enforce its requirements do not push these idioms to the point at which these paradoxes arise, the limits to which I have driven them in the previous chapters. From the standpoint of the salesperson, the commercial idiom and the service idiom do not have the status of conflicting theories or sets of propositions that are mutually inconsistent. On the contrary, they form interdependent practices that are linked in such a way that the performance of one is essential to the other. A close-driven sales program may, in theory, be inconsistent with a service-oriented program. In fact, however, commissions can be maximized only by serving clients' needs. These needs can be met most effectively not by well-meaning experts motivated exclusively by the client's welfare, but by sales personnel competitively motivated to achieve higher commissions. In theory, the success of a sale may depend upon the ability of the agent to control the sales process. In reality, the agent can achieve and maintain this control only by establishing a working consensus with the prospect.

Thus even if the sales process is a struggle for power over who controls the terms, logic, and direction of the interaction, the agent can prevail in this struggle only by gaining the trust of the prospect. This means that the agent must transpose the zero-sum conceptual apparatus of a competition in which one antagonist only can win into a joint consultation that leads to mutual agreement. Agents may engage in sales as a form of urban guerilla warfare in which success requires an aggressive, take-no-prisoners mentality, and they may be driven by the narrowest conception of self-interest imaginable. However, they can succeed often enough to return and do battle again only if they consistently meet certain expectations of the prospect. This means that the vulgar utilitarian ethic of pure self-interest must be tempered by a fiduciary ethic of professional responsibility. In the long run, success is possible only for agents whose self-interested motives include an interest in putting the prospect first. From the standpoint of the sales process as a theory constituted by an internally consistent set of propositions, this synthesis of the commercial idiom and the service idiom may be a self-contradictory absurdity. However, from the standpoint of the sales process as a practice—a collection of skills organized to realize the objective of high premiums and commissions—it is a necessity. Paradoxically, agents can exploit all their opportunities for sales only if they restrain their own opportunistic motives. The prospect's financial security needs must be elevated to a privileged status, where they remain untouched by the manipulative logic in which all things are reduced to instruments of the sales process. In short, agents can meet the demands of the commercial idiom only if they also respect the requirements of the service idiom.[73]

Suppose that the commercial idiom and the service idiom are abstracted from the sales process and formulated as theoretical statements. In that case, the propositions that express the essential premises of each idiom do, indeed, entail paradoxical consequences. However, the agent who operates within the sales process as a practice does not recognize these paradoxes. That is because they are produced by theoretical abstractions that are detached from the practice itself and the work experience of the agent. Therefore, they pose no dilemmas for the agent. Put another way, the commercial idiom and the service idiom, when driven back to their ultimate presuppositions by the theoretical transposition of the pragmatic rules of the sales process into two mutually inconsistent sets of premises, generate the antinomies outlined in the previous chapter. However, these antinomies do not arise within the practice of sales. This is because the sales process as a practice, rather than an object of theoretical reflection, does not employ either idiom rigorously or systematically. As a result, their mutual inconsistencies do not become visible within the work world of the agent.[74]

The foregoing remarks are based on a distinction between two different conceptions of personal sales. On the one hand, the sales process can be understood as a practice that is developed by personnel motivation specialists and marketing consultants, hammered into the sales force by sales managers, and applied by agents in the field. On the other hand, it can be regarded as an object of theoretical reflection by intellectuals who treat it as a set of doctrines that can be analyzed and criticized with regard to their truth content and mutual consistency. The paradoxical relationships between the commercial idiom and the service idiom do not appear in the world of work, governed by the practical articulation and execution of the sales process, but only in the world of theory, governed by reflection on the basic principles of the sales process.[75]

Agents do not conceive of the sales process as defined by propositions that are true or false, and thus potentially contradictory and mutually exclusive. On the contrary, they see it as governed by purely pragmatic rules of thumb. "Whatever works" is their ultimate dictum, which is agent shorthand for the rule: "Use whatever means can be expected to close the sale." Thus they do not think about the sales process from the perspective of its internal consistency, but rather from the standpoint of its practical efficacy and utility, as a means of maximizing commissions. Consistency and inconsistency are logical properties that can be ascribed only to propositions and their relationships. Therefore, a practice such as personal sales can be shown to be internally inconsistent only if it can be reduced to a set of propositions. It is also worth noting that only theories can be refuted on theoretical grounds. If the sales process is not a theory, then it cannot be disposed of by isolating putatively theoretical principles on which the commercial idiom and the service idiom are allegedly based and demonstrating their mutual inconsistencies.[76]

It could be said that the paradoxes of the sales process arise only if the commercial idiom and the service idiom are conceived of as distinct value spheres or autonomous domains of thought and action, each governed by its own definitive principles and subject to its own immanent norms. On this view, which we owe to Max Weber and Heinrich Rickert, "we are placed into different life spheres, each of which is governed by different laws."[77] As they develop, the value spheres of religion, ethics, politics, commerce, art, erotics, and science become increasingly autonomous. Each functions according to its own imperatives or quasi-nomological determinants.[78] However, from the standpoint of the logic that governs the work world of personal sales, the commercial idiom and the service idiom do not have the status of autonomous value spheres. Neither agents nor their managers theoretically extract the two idioms from the sales process and push them to their ultimate conclusions. As a result, the antinomies of the sales process are not part of their experience.

In my interviews with life insurance agents, questions about contradictions between the two idioms and attempts to demonstrate or illustrate any of the various antinomies of the sales process elicited two different responses. Some sales managers, general agents, and senior agents grasped the distinction between the two idioms immediately, even if they did not think about their own work in these terms. They responded to questions concerning possible conflicts between the two idioms by appealing to what they regard as a pre-established and self-evident harmony between "ethics" and "good business." In the long run, agents who prosper in the industry are able to link their own career interests to prospects' needs. Agents who "burn" prospects by employing deceitful and manipulative sales techniques may succeed in the short run. In the long run, they achieve a reputation for dishonesty, and thus their ability to survive in the business is limited.

Many agents, on the other hand, responded to these questions with a mixture of incomprehension and indifference. Selling is not something they theorize about, but something they do. Agents are trained to see selling as a craft and a technique. Although they discuss the sales process endlessly, it is hardly surprising that these discussions do not concern the principles that govern the process and the conditions for its coherence. Agent discussions of the sales process fall for the most part under the heading of shop talk, much of it technically sophisticated, laden with industry jargon, and consequently difficult for the outsider to follow. It is an eminently practical discourse about how to make things work, how to fine-tune technique, how to avoid pitfalls and mistakes, and how to hone personal selling skills most effectively.

If pragmatic questions about how to refine the sales process can be distinguished from reflexive questions about the principles on which the sales process is based, then my limited experience with agents suggests two conclusions. First, the occupational talk of most agents is limited to pragmatic issues. Second, when agents discuss questions on the reflexive level, the logic and rhetoric of their remarks are determined by industry ideology on the intimate relationship between sales and service—the platitudes and stereotypical formulae of training manuals and convention oratory.

The Limits of the Intellectualization of the Sales Process

These considerations pose a final question. Suppose that the antinomies of personal sales do not arise within the work experience of the agent. What factors are responsible for this? What means does the industry place at the agent's disposal for rendering the conflicts between the two idioms invisible? The sales process rests on fundamental contradictions that agents themselves do not perceive as such. What instruments does the industry employ to form the work world and perceptions of agents so that their effectiveness as sales personnel is not compromised by the paradoxes of the sales process? In response to this question and by way of conclusion, I should like to add four observations concerning linkages the industry establishes between the two idioms and how these linkages conceal the conflicts between them.

First, the sales process is underpinned and legitimized by the philosophy of financial security. As noted in chapter 3, this view holds that the ultimate purpose in life is to safeguard earning power, health, possessions, and dependents against the unpredictable assaults and shocks of fortune. Protection is achieved by purchasing the appropriate financial security instruments. The sales strategies and techniques of the commercial idiom are justified on the grounds of the indispensable contribution they make to the attainment of financial security. Agents are indoctrinated in this philosophy as part of their training. Indeed, their own commitment to this philosophy is held to be crucial to their success in the industry. Moreover, in purchasing insurance for themselves and protecting their own financial security, agents bear witness to the mutual consistency of the two idioms. In functioning as both producers and consumers of financial security products, agents testify to the interdependence of sales and service. Therefore, their own practice seems to eliminate the possibility of conflicts between them. In consequence, the philosophy of financial security makes it possible for agents to perform their occupational role without facing up to the conflicts it poses.

Second, the training process forms an occupational identity for the agent, as a result of which novitiates learn to conceive of their role as the critical variable in the equation that guarantees the financial security of the prospect. As noted in chapter 3, the sales process rests on the assumption that prospects generally have only a dim awareness of their true financial security needs. Although prospects may have considered in the most vague and uncertain terms what these needs are—for example, providing enough money to protect their dependents and to secure a respectable retirement— the decision to act on these needs is frequently compromised by other considerations: an interest in current consumption and the inability to save; intellectual laziness and the unwillingness to work out what is required by financial security; and moral irresponsibility and the failure to consider how the security of dependents will be adversely affected by the interruption or termination of the prospect's earning power. More often than not, prospects have no conception of the range and quality of the products available to meet their needs. They lack the knowledge required to make an intelligent purchasing decision and the discipline necessary to execute a long-term financial security plan. The role of the agent is to advise and guide prospects: to provide assistance in articulating and prioritizing their financial security needs; to encourage prospects to take these needs seriously and meet their responsibilities to dependents; to lead prospects through the confusing world of financial security products and help them choose the instrument best suited to their problems and situation; and finally, to coach prospects in developing the disciplines that will maintain their financial security plan intact. Thus the identity of the agent is based on the assumption that his or her own sales efforts are essential to the financial security of the prospect. Because the work of the agent appears to demonstrate the dependence of the service idiom on the commercial idiom—the prospect's financial security interests can be secured only by means of the commercially oriented efforts of the agent—the possibility of conflicts between the two idioms is obscured.

Third, as noted in chapter 2, criteria for the retention, remuneration, promotion, and termination of agents are strictly quantitative. For the agent, there is a strong sense in which everything depends upon "making your numbers." Invitations to annual conventions, with the costs of travel and accommodation covered by the company, membership in the Million Dollar Roundtable, and the other indices and tokens of prestige and advancing status in the industry are all tied to the premiums the agent is expected to produce according to a prescribed schedule. At the other extreme, the agent who persistently fails to deliver a certain amount of business to the company each month will not survive. According to the sales process, making your numbers is a function of the way you spend your time: the number of prospecting calls you make, the number of referred leads you pursue, and the number of interviews you conduct, all of which determine the number of sales you close and, ultimately, the amount of premium you produce.

As the agent learns, spending time on the job does not necessarily mean working harder. It means working "smarter." Agents who work smarter devote themselves to improving their skills and sharpening their sales technique. In this way, they minimize the chances of offending a prospect, bungling the opportunity to get a referred lead, slipping up in an interview, or committing a blunder during the all-important attempt to close the sale. Working smarter, in other words, means thinking on the pragmatic level: reading industry publications on sales technique, attending seminars on how to improve performance in the various phases of the sales process, practicing skills, and discussing performance problems with other agents. Agents who work smarter use their time effectively instead of wasting it. From the standpoint of the sales process, time is wasted when it is devoted to non-instrumental activities that make no contribution to the agent's sales performance. Thus reflexive discourse is a waste of time. Agents who employ their time pondering the conflicts between the commercial idiom and the service idiom and reflecting on the various antinomies of the sales process are not engaged in productive work. What is worse, indulgence in reflexive thought can be expected to produce deficits in peformance. It cannot be supposed that agents who see through the sales process to the contradictions on which it rests and grasp the consequences of these contradictions for their work will prove capable of maintaining the hearty self-confidence and cheerful poise that are said to be essential in confronting prospects.

Thus it could be said that from the standpoint of agent survival, the sales process functions as a selection mechanism. It operates in favor of agents whose reflections are confined to the instrumental and pragmatic level, and it selects against those who engage in reflexive thought. Consider two agents, A^1 and A^2, competing for the same prospect, P. Suppose that A^1 is a pure pragmatist who devotes all his or her energies to the improvement of sales technique. Suppose that A^2 reserves some part of his or her time for noninstrumental reflections on the meaning of the sales process and the paradoxes it generates. Because A^2 will suffer the deficits in performance that result from these reflections, the sales process selects in favor of A^1 and against A^2. In the long run this means that, other considerations remaining the same, agents who indulge in reflexive thought will be eliminated from the industry by their more pragmatically and instrumentally oriented competitors.

Finally, consider the conception of the sales process as a selection mechanism that rewards pragmatic reflection as working smarter and penalizes reflexive contemplation as not working at all. This view is powerfully reinforced by the rites to which the agent is subjected at company conventions. From the standpoint of the care and feeding of the sales force, the convention functions essentially as a legitimation ritual and a celebration of success.[79] When agents are asked to survey their careers, they frequently recall annual conventions as the major landmarks that document and certify their success or, as the case may be, their failures. The hotel suite and the dinner with the company president tend to be remembered as especially impressive features of the convention experience. One agent recalls his first major convention.

> In 1980, I was third or fourth in the country in life insurance sales for my company. We went to Disney World, where the convention took place. I was, I think, only twenty-five at the time. I was part of what was called "The President's Club." Which means you get to the convention a little ahead of time. The big hitters—that's what they call them—and the new young studs get there two days ahead of time. And the first thing is they give me this huge suite. They give me the key. And my wife and I open the door to this thing. It's an honest-to-God apartment. Waiting for us on the table in the living room is this big bowl of fruit and champagne and stuff from the president of the company, with his compliments and an invitation to have dinner with him at his table. You know, I was rather nervous about the whole thing. In any case, my wife and I became hysterical looking over this suite, which was about the size of our own apartment in those days.

The same agent remembers the presidential dinner at the same convention.

We go to this dinner. I was seated up front at the big table with the company president. The point of this dinner, essentially, is to make us feel good, especially a young, up-and-coming person like myself. What they did was, they sat us next to people who were the big hitters. They wouldn't let you sit with your wife. I ended up sitting next to this guy from Texas who sells more insurance than anybody in our company. All he talked about was how you sell more insurance. The president gave a big pep talk first. Then each of the big producers had to stand up for applause.

Agents who devote themselves systematically and unremittingly to the disciplines of the sales process make their numbers and produce the volume of sales required to qualify for the convention. At this assemblage, they are congratulated for performing in precisely the ways that are responsible for their presence there. Another agent offers the following observations on the convention experience.

They hired one of these promotional organizations to put on a show. The room would go black. Right? And we're all sitting there. It's really like a bad movie in a way. In any case, this patriotic American music would start playing. Very loud. Then eagles would be flashing on the walls. American eagles would show up and American flags. Then we go into the insurance thing, and they show pictures, basically of big achievers. In other words, the theme was: "Anyone can make it. You, of course, have made it. That's why you're here." Then the lights go on, and the president of the company stands up and gives a long talk. It was all very moralistic. You know: "America is a great place, and insurance is a great business." Then they had an invocation, a prayer just before dinner. This is where Jesus Christ was invoked to help us sell more insurance.

New and promising agents as well as experienced high achievers are celebrated in reward ceremonies and cheered on by motivational speakers. One agent remarks on the prominent role that convention planners reserve for motivational speakers, who are engaged as free-lance specialists in inspiration.

The motivational speakers are very important. These guys are taken extremely seriously. There's the super-salesman who made millions of dollars selling insurance and then makes millions telling you how he did it. Then there are speakers drawn from the military. This is very interesting. This one guy was an MIA who had come back from Vietnam and was still active. Anyway, we always had military people there. By the way, this particular guy I've seen on these religious pentecostal shows on tv, giving the same speech verbatim. He gave a speech, the theme of which was self-confidence. The guy gets shot down over Vietnam. He gets captured by the North Vietnamese. He talks about how he communicated by knocking on the walls. We've all heard this story. But how did he make it back? And what does this have to do with sales? He made it back through belief in God and belief in America. And what do we mean by America? We mean the ability to do what insurance salesmen can do, the ability to be nothing and become something. It was great, great stuff to look at from this angle. But he had an entire audience of hard-core salesmen in the palm of his hand. I mean when he stopped talking he got a standing ovation for over five minutes.[80]

Both agents and their families are showered with prizes, perquisites, and entertainments that testify to their success. The consistent lesson of the convention is that success and prestige are tied to the pragmatic mode of discourse. Agents who engage in reflexive thought are not charged with weakness and defeatism. At the convention, they are not even mentioned. It is as if they did not exist, a wordless condemnation to the social hell reserved for those whose identity has been forgotten. Thus the message of the convention—pounded into the agent in a heady emotional atmosphere that combines elements of televangelism, Las Vegas lounge acts, the Miss America Pageant, and television game shows—produces powerful sanctions that reconfirm the industry theory of the sales process as a seamless synthesis of commerce and service.

On the one hand, it is true that the sales process intellectualizes the life of the agent. On the other hand, the intellectualization of life is pursued only in a certain direction, within certain limits, and only in the interest of certain values. Other orientations and values are neglected or nullified. The sales process forms the life of the agent as a series of technical problems: how to recruit prospects most effectively, how to develop referred leads without wasting valuable prospecting time, how to conduct successful sales interviews, how to close a prospect. For fully trained agents, life is a series of technical challenges that are attacked in a certain sequence and solved by means of certain preferred methods. The kind of thinking required to master the sales process is pragmatic and instrumental, not reflexive. Thought is translated into instrumental calculation and geared to the production of sales results. The intellectualization of the life of the agent in the direction of greater sales productivity excludes reflection on the principles of the sales process as a nonproductive or counterproductive waste of time.

In sum, agents who can stand up under the stresses and anxieties of the life insurance business and survive in the industry cannot be expected to see through the logic of the sales process to the contradictions on which it rests. Such a vision would destroy their effectiveness by shattering the illusions on which their careers depend.

Notes

1. Leslie Aldridge Westoff, "As Incentive, Anything Goes," *The Business World: The New York Times Magazine*, April 2, 1989, p. 81.
2. Ibid.
3. See, for example, Richard H. Buskirk, *Principles of Marketing* (New York: Holt, Rinehart and Winston, 1970); Gilbert A. Churchill Jr., Neil M. Ford, and Orville C. Walker Jr., *Sales Force Management* (Homewood, IL.: Richard D. Irwin, 1981); U. Grant Marsh, *Salesmanship* (Englewood Cliffs, NJ: Prentice-Hall, 1972); Charles D. Schewe and Reuben M. Smith, *Marketing: Concepts and Applications* (New York: McGraw-Hill, 1980); and William J. Stanton and Richard H. Buskirk, *Management of the Sales Force* (Homewood, IL.: Richard D. Irwin, 1983). The key article in the development of this concept is Robert N. McMurry, "The Mystique of Super-Salesmanship, *Harvard Business Review* 39 (1961):113–23.
4. On direct selling organizations, see Nicole Woolsey Biggart, *Charismatic Capitalism: Direct Selling Organizations in America* (Chicago: University of Chicago Press, 1989).
5. F. William Howton and Bernard Rosenberg, "The Salesman: Ideology and Self-Imagery in a Prototypic Occupation," *Social Research* 32 (1965):277–98. On the same point, see Robert C. Prus, *Pursuing Customers: An Ethnography of Marketing Activities* (Newbury Park, CA: Sage Publications, 1989), pp. 30–32. For some recent exceptions to this generalization, see Susan Porter Benson, *Counter Cultures: Saleswomen, Managers, and Customers in American Department Stores, 1890–1940* (Urbana, IL.: University of Illinois Press, 1988); Biggart, *Charismatic Capitalism*; Robert C. Prus, *Making Sales: Influence as Interpersonal Accomplishment* (Newbury Park, CA: Sage Publications, 1989); and Viviana A. Rotman Zelizer, *Morals and Markets: The Development of Life Insurance in the United States* (New York: Columbia University Press, 1979).
6. For examples of this literature, with extensive bibliographies, see Michael Burawoy, *Manufacturing Consent: Changes in the Labor Process under Monopoly Capitalism* (Chicago: University of Chicago Press, 1979); Milton Cantor (ed.), *American Workingclass Culture* (Westport, CT: Greenwood, 1979); Ken Kusterer, *Know-How on the Job: The Important Knowledge of "Unskilled" Workers* (Boulder: Westview Replication Press, 1978); and Daniel Nelson, *Managers and Workers: Origins of the New Factory System in the United States* (Madison: University of Wisconsin Press, 1975).
7. For recent examples of this literature, see Howard E. Aldrich, *Organizations and Environments* (Englewood Cliffs, NJ: Prentice-Hall, 1979); John Meyer and W. Richard Scott, *Organizational Ritual and Rationality* (Beverly Hills, CA: Sage Publications, 1983); and W. Richard Scott, *Organizations: Rational, Natural, and Open Systems* (Englewood Cliffs, NJ: Prentice-Hall, 1981).
8. See JoAnn Gennaro Gora and Gloria Nemerowicz, *Emergency Squad Volunteers* (New York: Praeger, 1985); Arlie Russell Hochschild, *The Managed Heart: The*

99

Commercialization of Human Feeling (Berkeley: University of California Press, 1983); Paul C. P. Siu, *The Chinese Laundryman* (New York: New York University Press, 1987); James Spradley and Brenda Mann, *Cocktail Waitress* (New York: Random House, 1975); and Linda Valli, *Becoming Clerical Workers* (Boston: Routledge & Kegan Paul, 1986).

9. For a recent critical survey of research on professions, see Robert Dingwell and Philip Lewis (eds.), *The Sociology of the Professions* (London: Macmillan, 1983).

10. See especially Robert Jackall, *Moral Mazes: the World of Corporate Managers* (New York: Oxford University Press, 1988) and the literature cited in his "Suggestions for Further Reading."

11. C. Wright Mills, "The Great Salesroom," pp. 161–88 in *White Collar* (New York: Oxford University Press, 1951). It cannot be assumed that the conclusions supported by a sociology of corporate management will also hold for sales personnel. Consider, for example, Jackall's study of corporate managers, *Moral Mazes*. As Jackall claims, it is true that sales, like managerial work and other white collar work, has become increasingly bureaucratized. However, many of the conclusions he reaches concerning the occupational ethics of managers are not valid for the work world of personal sales. Sales personnel are not subject to the obligations of unconditional loyalty that managers owe to their bosses, nor are the long-run career chances of sales personnel tied to the performance of fealty obligations to their managers. In the social organization of the sales force, credit and social honor do not emanate from the sales manager down to the sales force. On the contrary, the income of sales managers is tied to "overrides" drawn from the commissions of the sales personnel they manage, and sales managers' jobs depend upon the performance of the sales personnel they recruit. Thus the reverse relation is closer to the truth. Because the occupational fate of sales personnel is determined by their ability to meet sales quotas, they tend not to be plagued by the anxieties about "organizational contingency" that Jackall ascribes to managers. As we shall see, the work world of personal sales creates its own distinctive anxieties. However, they are not primarily a consequence of uncertain relations between sales personnel and their managers. The indeterminacy between performance and reward that Jackall finds in managerial work does not hold in personal sales. From the standpoint of criteria for success in personal sales, meeting monthly sales quotas is not the major consideration; it is the only consideration. Finally, the organization of a sales force does not encourage scapegoating. Consistently high performers need never fear that they will be held responsible for the mistakes of their managers.

12. See Robert Ketchum Bain, "The Process of Professionalization: Life Insurance Selling," Ph.D. dissertation, University of Chicago, 1959; J. Owen Stalson, *Marketing Life Insurance* (Bryn Mawr, PA: McCahan Foundation, 1969 [1942]); and Zelizer, *Morals and Markets*.

13. *Life Association News*, August 1988, p. 39; July 1989, p. 32.

14. On the Armstrong Commission hearings, see Stalson, *Marketing Life Insurance*.

15. Interviewees are responsible for all emphases in material quoted from interviews. Material in brackets is added by the author.

16. *Let's Do Something about Prospecting* (Hartford, CT.: LIMRA, 1985), p. 45.

17. *The Pilot's Log*, summer 1988, p. 39.

18. *Let's Do Something about Prospecting*, p. 13. For some general observations on the

role of prospecting in personal sales, see Prus, *Pursuing Customers*, pp. 243–76.

19. Erving Goffman, *Relations in Public* (New York: Basic Books, 1971), p. 372.

20. One of the first exercises of the agent-in-training is to complete a list of one hundred names of such acquaintances and "qualify" them from the standpoint of income, age, occupation, and ability to generate business. For an amusing but deadly accurate and merciless depiction of the importance of these lists in personal sales, see David Mamet's phenomenology of everyday life in real estate sales, *Glenngarry Glenn Ross* (New York: The Grove Press, 1984).

21. Chuck Jones, "Tips to Keep You in Business," *Life Association News*, March 1988, p. 74.

22. D. Forbes Ley, "Shake up a Prospect and He Becomes a Client," *Life Association News*, April 1989, p. 44.

23. Ibid. Agents have an acute sense of the role of women as consumers of life insurance, both as primary purchasers of policies and also as wives who collaborate with the agent to guarantee the success of a sale to their husbands. According to one agent, "It's fatal to ignore the wife."

> Follow-up calling, for instance. What's the best way to do it? As women are becoming more integrated into the economic system, it's very clear that insurance companies are gearing more of their business to women. In the early 80s, a lot of these guys would laughingly say: "You gotta get ahold of the wife. Don't ever call the man. He'll just put you off. Tell the wife that her husband hasn't paid the premium. That almost guarantees it will be paid." So you attack on that level, by hitting the wife, and make sure that the sale stays sold.

Although women are regarded as increasingly important consumers of life insurance, the industry itself remains a bastion of male domination. This is reflected in occupational statistics. According to LIMRA demographics, only thirteen percent of full-time agents are women (*Life Association News*, July 1989, p. 67). It is also expressed in the informal rhetoric of the work world of the agent, which is embellished with the phallocentric idioms of middle-class-male bar-and-locker-room patois.

24. Jack E. Bobo, "Viewpoint," *Life Association News*, April 1989, p. 13.

25. David P. Dashner, "What Do You Say to Someone in Mourning?," *Life Association News*, April 1989, p. 154.

26. For suggestions along these lines—techniques of impression management to be employed on prospects suffering extreme emotional distress caused by the death of a loved one—see ibid.

27. B. Wilks, *Prudential Training Program: X-PAR Prospecting System* (Newark, NJ: PruPress, 1986), p. 32.

28. Ibid., p. 36.

29. Ibid., p. 37.

30. Ibid., p. 42.

31. Ibid., p. 41.

32. Steven F. Sullivan, "Attracting Clients and How to Hold Them," *Life Association News*, March 1987, pp. 90, 93.

33. Chuck Jones, "The Plan's the Thing," *Life Association News*, December 1988, p. 80.

34. Joe Razza Jr., "Sales Tips You Can Use Today," *Life Association News*, January 1988, p. 90.

35. Wilks, *Prudential Training Program*, p. 39.
36. See J. Michael Stevens, "Measuring a Successful Agent," *Life Association News*, March 1989, pp. 126–27.
37. Georg Simmel, "The Metropolis and Mental Life," p. 414, in *The Sociology of Georg Simmel*, translated and edited, with an introduction, by Kurt H. Wolff (New York: The Free Press, 1964).
38. There is a substantial and somewhat inchoate literature on the textualization of social phenomena. See, for example, Richard Harvey Brown, *Society as Text* (Chicago: University of Chicago Press, 1987); Clifford Geertz, *The Interpretation of Culture* (New York: Basic Books, 1973) and *Local Knowledge: Further Essays in Interpretive Anthropology* (New York: Basic Books, 1983); Paul Ricoeur, "The Model of the Text: Meaningful Action Considered as a Text," pp. 197–221, in *Hermeneutics and the Human Sciences*, translated and edited, with an introduction, by John D. Thompson (New York: Cambridge University Press, 1981); and Peter Winch, *The Idea of a Social Science* (London: Routledge & Kegan Paul, 1958). The abbreviated position I develop in the above discussion may be compared with Edward Said's comprehensive analysis of the textual constitution of the Orient by Western explorers, colonial administrators, and orientalists in *Orientalism* (New York: Pantheon, 1978).
39. See Harry Braverman, *Labor and Monopoly Capitalism: The Degradation of Work in the Twentieth Century* (New York: Monthly Review Press, 1974), and Richard Edwards, *Contested Terrain: The Transformation of the Workplace in the Twentieth Century* (New York: Basic Books, 1979).
40. According to the 1988 LIMRA survey, agents with an average of twelve years' experience reported annual median earnings of $52,000. See *The Pilot's Log*, summer 1988, p. 39.
41. The thesis of the degradation of employee skills produced by advanced managerial capitalism has been defended by students of industrial labor. For additional arguments that this thesis cannot be extended without qualification to the work process characteristic of modern service industries, see Barbara Melosh, *"The Physician's Hand": Work, Culture, and Conflict in American Nursing* (Philadelphia: Temple University Press, 1982), and Benson, *Counter Cultures.*
42. On this point, see William Leiss, *The Limits of Satisfaction: An Essay on the Problem of Needs and Commodities* (Toronto: University of Toronto Press, 1976), pp. 13–28.
43. Major life insurance companies occasionally attempt to identify the value priorities of potential consumers of their products and determine how these priorities are formed. See, for example, the survey of American values in the 1980s commissioned by the Connecticut Mutual Life Insurance Company: *The Connecticut Mutual Life Report on American Values in the 80s: The Impact of Belief* (Hartford, CT: Connecticut Mutual Life Insurance Company, 1981).
44. Research on professions exhibits a number of different tendencies and interests. There is a relatively unimaginative strategy that analyzes professions by reference to the traits or attributes that are alleged to constitute a profession. This research approximates quite closely the above sketch of professionalism as it is conceived in the life insurance industry. Among the many examples of this genre, see William J. Goode, "Community within a Community: The Profes-

sions," *American Sociological Review* 22 (1957):194–200, and "Encroachment, Charlatanism, and the Emerging Profession: Psychology, Medicine, and Sociology," *American Sociological Review* 25 (1960):902–14; Ernest Greenwood, "Attributes of a Profession," *Social Work* 2 (1957):44–55; and Wilbert E. Moore, *The Professions: Roles and Rules* (New York: Russell Sage, 1970). Talcott Parsons' analysis of professions was developed within the context of his theory of the normative order of modern capitalist societies. According to this theory, the social order of complex societies cannot be accounted for on the basis of marginal utility theory or utilitarian principles of self-interest maximization. On the contrary, it presupposes standards that define a normative order. Parsons regarded his analysis of the professions as a confirmation of this general theory of the social order. See, for example, Talcott Parsons, "The Professions and Social Structure," pp. 34–49, in *Essays in Sociological Theory*, revised edition (New York: The Free Press, 1954). Everett Hughes' analysis of professions is a part of his theory of occupations in modern societies and the ways occupations articulate the division of labor and develop its consequences. See, for example, Everett C. Hughes, *Men and Their Work* (Glencoe: The Free Press, 1958), and *The Sociological Eye* (Chicago: Aldine, 1971). The phenomenon of professional socialization is analyzed in two classical works: Howard Becker et al., *Boys in White* (Chicago: University of Chicago Press, 1961), and Robert K. Merton et al., *The Student Physician* (Cambridge: Harvard University Press, 1957). On the ways professions are linked to the stratification system and the market for professional services, see M. S. Larson, *The Rise of Professionalism: A Sociological Analysis* (Berkeley: University of California Press, 1977). On the relations between professionals and political and economic elites, see T. J. Johnson, *Professions and Power* (London: Macmillan, 1972). On the political influence of professions and the role of political power in the process by which occupational groups attempt to sustain their claim to professional status, see Eliot Friedson, *The Profession of Medicine* (New York: Harper & Row, 1970). On the relationship between professional and bureaucratic principles for the organization of work, see Celia Davies, "Professionals in Bureaucracies: The Conflict Thesis Revised," pp. 177–93 in Dingwell and Lewis, *Sociology of the Professions*. For two useful critical surveys of the literature on professions, see Eliot Friedson, "The Theory of Professions: State of the Art," ibid., pp. 19–37, and Dietrich Rueschemeyer, "Professional Autonomy and the Social Control of Expertise," ibid., pp. 38–58. On the development of the professional ideal in modern culture, see Burton J. Bledstein, *The Culture of Professionalism* (New York: Norton, 1976), and W. J. Reader, *Professional Men: The Rise of the Professional Classes in Nineteenth Century England* (London: Weidenfeld and Nicolson, 1966).

45. On the ambivalence of industry literature concerning the esteem in which agents and their work is held, see *New England Life Associate's Career Track*, unit I, module 1 (Boston: New England Life, 1983). On the low occupational prestige and "occupational stigma" that attach to life insurance sales, see Zelizer, *Morals and Markets*, pp. 134–40. Zelizer borrows Erving Goffman's concept of stigma to elucidate the sense in which life insurance agents are contaminated by the "dirty work" of making money out of death. See Erving Goffman, *Stigma* (Englewood Cliffs, NJ: Prentice-Hall, 1963). On the low

prestige of personal sales in general, see John L. Mason, "The Low Prestige of Personal Selling," *Journal of Marketing* 29 (1965):7–10, and Prus, *Making Sales,* pp. 262–63.

46. Thomas J. Wolff, *Financial Need Analysis Sales Manual* (Vernon, CT: Vernon Publishing Services, 1983), p. 10.

47. The ensuing discussion depends heavily on Max Weber's analysis of salvation religions. See especially Max Weber, *Economy and Society,* edited by Guenther Roth and Claus Wittich (Berkeley: University of California Press, 1978), Chapter 6, pp. 399–634; "The Social Psychology of the World Religions," pp. 267–301 in *From Max Weber: Essays in Sociology,* translated, edited, and with an introduction by H. H. Gerth and C. Wright Mills (New York: Oxford University Press, 1958); and "Religious Rejections of the World and Their Directions," ibid., pp. 323–59. On the marketing and consumption of goods and services as expressions of a conception of the world in which the identities of salesperson and prospect are defined beyond the purely instrumental realm of sales, see also Mary Douglas and Baron Isherwood, *The World of Goods* (New York: Basic Books, 1979), and Biggart, *Charismatic Capitalism,* pp. 114–16.

48. On the "bearers" or purveyors of conceptions of the world as intellectuals, see Weber, *Economy and Society,* Chapter 6, pp. 399–634; "The Social Psychology of the World Religions"; and "Religious Rejections of the World and Their Directions." See also Antonio Gramsci, "The Intellectuals," pp. 5–23 in *Selections from the Prison Notebooks,* edited and translated by Quintin Hoare and Geoffrey Nowell Smith (New York: International Publishers, 1971).

   Formally and conceptually, the philosophy of financial security represents a secularized, individualized, and privatized reconfiguration of the New England "errand" or mission of seventeenth-century Puritanism and its stress on salvation as achieved by a dual strategy of activism and self-denial. The sales methods of life insurance agents who market the philosophy of financial security also parallel in interesting ways the rhetoric of Puritan homiletics. New England divines relied upon spiritual biographies to provide ideal types of the Christian life and its progress from unregenerate worldliness to spiritual conversion, resistance to temptation, and commitment to regenerate living. In the same way, life insurance agents exploit "success stories" of what can be achieved by the philosophy of financial security in the hands of the prospects they convert. Torn by financial anxiety and uncertainty, converts see the light of insurance and achieve redemption through effective financial planning and the struggle against irrational consumption. On the New England "errand," see Perry Miller, *Errand into the Wilderness* (Cambridge, MA: Harvard University Press, 1956); Sacvan Bercovitch, *The Puritan Origins of the American Self* (New Haven: Yale University Press, 1975), *The American Jeremiad* (Madison: University of Wisconsin Press, 1978), and "New England's Errand Reappraised," pp. 85–104 in John Higham and Paul K. Conkin (eds.), *New Directions in American Intellectual History* (Baltimore: Johns Hopkins University Press, 1979). On the rhetoric of Puritan homiletics and its use of spiritual life stories, see Bercovitch, *The Puritan Origins of the American Self,* pp. 23–25.

49. *New England Life Associate's Career Track,* unit I, module 6 (Boston: New England Life, 1983), p. 38.

50. *Prepare to Sell* (Hartford, CT: LIMRA, 1984), p. 11.

51. On these two aspects of trust, see Bernard Barber, *The Logic and Limits of Trust* (New Brunswick: Rutgers University Press, 1983), pp. 14–21.
52. C. Miller, *Prudential Training Program: The Financial Security Selling System,* Book 1 (Newark, NJ: PruPress, 1986), p. 15. On the prospect's willingness to trust the salesperson—or, what amounts to the same thing, the salesperson's ability to demonstrate trustworthiness—as a necessary condition for closing sales, see Prus, *Making Sales,* pp. 102–30. For recent marketing literature in this area, see F. Robert Dwyer et al., "Developing Buyer-Seller Relationships," *Journal of Marketing* 51 (1987): 11–27; Jon Hawes et al., "Trust Earning Perceptions of Sellers and Buyers," *Journal of Personal Selling and Sales Management* 9 (1989): 1–8; Paul Schurr and Julie Ozanne, "Influences on Exchange Processes: Buyers' Preconceptions of a Seller's Trustworthiness and Bargaining Toughness," *Journal of Consumer Research* 11 (1985): 939–53; and John Swan and Johannah Nolan, "Gaining Customer Trust: A Conceptual Guide for the Salesperson," *Journal of Personal Selling and Sales Management* 5 (1985): 39–48.
53. On trust and the inability to monitor the actions of others, see Partha Dasgupta, "Trust as a Commodity," pp. 49–72 in Diego Gambetta (ed.), *Trust* (New York: Blackwell, 1988).
54. This paragraph draws on Bernard Williams, "Formal Structures and Social Reality," pp. 3–13 in Gambetta, *Trust.*
55. Niklas Luhmann, "Familiarity, Confidence, Trust: Problems and Alternatives," p. 95 in Gambetta, *Trust.*
56. C. Miller, *Prudential Training Program,* Book 1, p. 15.
57. W. Walsh, *Prudential Training Program: Salesmanship and Selling* (Newark, NJ: PruPress, 1986), p. 15.
58. On the relation between secrecy and trust, see Simmel, "The Secret Society," pp. 345–48 in *The Sociology of Georg Simmel.*
59. Lesley E. Weiner, "Financial Plan Provides Sales Roadmap," *The Pilot's Log,* summer 1988, p. 8.
60. On the analysis of role conflicts in general, see Robert House and John Rizzo, "Role Conflict and Ambiguity as Critical Variables in a Model of Organizational Behavior," *Organizational Behavior and Human Performance* 7 (1972): 467–505; Robert L. Kahn et al., *Organizational Stress: Studies in Role Conflicts and Ambiguity* (New York: Wiley, 1964); and John Rizzo et al., "Role Conflict and Ambiguity in Complex Organizations," *Administrative Science* 15 (1970): 150–63. For a useful analysis of the theoretical literature in this area, see Mary Van Sell et al., "Role Conflict and Role Ambiguity: Integration of the Literature and Directions for Future Research," *Human Relations* 34 (1981): 43–71.
61. For the sociological literature on the contradictions inherent in personal sales, see Benson, *Counter Cultures;* Joy Browne, *The Used-Car Game: A Sociology of the Bargain* (Lexington, MA: Lexington Books); Howton and Rosenberg, "The Salesman"; Prus, *Making Sales;* and Zelizer, *Morals and Markets.* For the marketing literature, see Douglas Behrman et al., "Sources of Job Related Ambiguity and Their Consequences upon Salespersons' Job Satisfaction and Performance," *Management Science* 27 (1981): 1246–60; L. R. Chonko, "The Relationship of Span of Control to Sales Representatives' Experienced Role Conflict and Role Ambiguity," *Academy of Management Journal* 25 (1982): 452–56; Alan Dubinsky and Thomas Ingram, "Correlates of Salespeople's Ethical Conflicts: An Explor-

atory Investigation," *Journal of Business Ethics* 3 (1984): 343–53; Louis Fry et al., "An Analysis of Alternative Causal Models of Salesperson Role Perceptions and Work-Related Attitudes," *Journal of Marketing Research* 23 (1986): 153–63; and R. Kenneth Teas et al., "A Path Analysis of Causes and Consequences of Salespeoples' Perceptions of Role Clarity," *Journal of Marketing Research* 16 (1979): 355–69.

62. On the conflict between the imperatives of a professional ethic and the demands of a bureaucratic or corporate ethic, see Jackall, *Moral Mazes*.

63. On emotional work, see Hochschild, *Managed Heart*. On the occupational control of emotion, see Carol Zisowitz Stearns and Peter N. Stearns, *Anger: The Struggle for Emotional Control in America's History* (Chicago: University of Chicago Press, 1986), especially pp. 170–73.

64. On the concept of sincerity, see Lionel Trilling, *Sincerity and Authenticity* (Cambridge, MA: Harvard University Press, 1972). On the fallacy involved in the attempt to demonstrate the possession of qualities such as sincerity, in which the intentionality of the demonstration nullifies its aim or object, see Jon Elster, "States That are Essentially By-Products," pp. 43–108 in *Sour Grapes: Studies in the Subversion of Rationality* (New York: Cambridge University Press, 1985). This fallacy can be characterized in the following terms. Suppose that the desired state of sincerity depends upon an absence of intentionality, calculation, or striving. In that case, an attempt to achieve sincerity by intentional effort or deliberation is self-defeating. That is because any such attempt renders impossible the result it proposes to accomplish.

65. On the relation between the salesperson and the entertainer, see Howton and Rosenberg, "The Salesman." On the dramaturgic qualities of social interaction, see Richard Harvey Brown, *A Poetic for Sociology* (New York: Cambridge University Press, 1977); Erving Goffman, *The Presentation of Self in Everyday Life* (Garden City, NY: Doubleday, 1959); Stanford Lyman and Marvin Scott, *The Drama of Social Reality* (New York: Oxford University Press, 1975); and Victor Turner, *Dramas, Fields, and Metaphors* (Ithaca, NY: Cornell University Press, 1974), and "Social Dramas and Stories about Them," *Critical Inquiry,* autumn 1980: 141–68.

66. For a useful if turgid analysis of the relations between trust, complexity, and unpredictability, see Niklas Luhmann, *Trust and Power* (New York: Wiley, 1979), especially pp. 15, 24–25, 39, 43, 62–63.

67. In light of the above discussion of the ways opportunism defeats trust, reconsider the use of friends as prospects or sources of referred leads. It is, of course, true that friendship may rest on the fact that we enjoy the company of certain people. We also generally rely on friends for services, and we perform services for them in return, either because of the value we place on what our friends do for us or because of the place they fill in our lives. However, friendship involves more than a merely instrumental relation based on mutual advantage. Although the essential features of friendship can be characterized in different ways, two features seem especially important. First, my friendship with other persons depends upon my concern for their welfare. I am willing to pursue the well-being of my friends simply because they are my friends and regardless of the advantages this may produce for me. In other words, friendship entails mutual cares and concerns that differentiate it from other relationships and exceed what

people generally expect from one another. Second, friendship also involves a mutual trust that makes it possible to reveal ourselves to our friends more completely and profoundly than holds true in our other relationships. Because of this trust, we divulge to friends matters we conceal from others, and we discuss with friends intimate personal concerns that we might not broach even with members of our own families. What is responsible for the trust between friends? It is not due merely to the fact that we know our friends will prove helpful and sympathetic in talking over these matters. We also know that they will not violate the confidence we place in them. For an extended analysis of friendship that stresses these two aspects of the relationship—concern for the well-being of the friend and the elements of trust and intimacy—see Lawrence A. Blum, *Friendship, Altruism and Morality* (London: Routledge & Kegan Paul, 1980).

In view of these considerations, training programs in sales that stress the employment of friends as both prospects and sources of referred leads seem misguided on several counts. Most obviously, the reduction of other persons to prospects involves using them as tools. This is inconsistent with the ethic of friendship, which requires that we value our friends for their own sake, not for the contribution they make to the fulfillment of sales quotas. Agents who use friends as prospects violate their own friendships and debase the relation of friendship itself. Techniques for the use of friends as sources of referred leads also depend upon conduct that is inconsistent with friendship: deceit, trickery, and manipulation. Finally, consider the use of friends as sources of referred leads to their own friends. This practice presupposes that the agent's friends will violate the trust that their friends have placed them by revealing confidential matters to a third party—the agent. Thus, referees are encouraged to violate their friendships in the same way that agents have compromised their friendships with these same referees. In sum, the sales process, which requires the agent to employ all persons and exploit all relationships as sources of potential prospects, is inconsistent with the possibility of friendship. Put another way, the sales process debases the friendships it employs by translating them into commercial relationships. Since friendship is the relationship that agents are trained to exploit most aggressively, it follows that the sales process is self-defeating in yet another respect. On the one hand, it encourages agents to use their friends as prospects and sources of referred leads. This tactic takes advantage of the fact that our friends have an unselfish interest in our welfare. It is not necessary to motivate them to act on our behalf. On the other hand, in putting friends to these uses, agents destroy the very friendships they attempt to exploit, thereby compromising their most important source of prospects.

68. Max Weber, "Science as a Vocation," p. 148 in *From Max Weber: Essays in Sociology*.
69. Ibid., p. 156.
70. F. Scott Fitzgerald, *The Crack-Up* (New York: New Directions, 1956), p. 69.
71. Friedrich Nietzsche, *The Will to Power*, translated by Walter Kaufmann and R. J. Hollingdale (New York: Random House, 1968), no. 609.
72. The general point at issue here—that institutions cannot exist without illusions—is essential to Nietzsche's conception of "untruth as a condition for life." See, for example, *Beyond Good and Evil*, translated by Walter Kaufmann (New

York: Vintage, 1966), p. 39; *Daybreak*, translated by R. J. Hollingdale (New York: Cambridge University Press, 1982), p. 507; and *The Gay Science*, translated by Walter Kaufmann (New York: Vintage, 1974), pp. 344, 347. For a useful analysis of Nietzsche's conception of the relations between life and illusions, see Alexander Nehamas, *Nietzsche: Life as Literature* (Cambridge, MA: Harvard University Press, 1985), especially pp. 69–70.

73. From time to time, the industry takes special efforts to remind agents of these practical truths and their foundation in the dependence of the commercial idiom on the service idiom. Recently, the *Life Association News* made this dependence the major theme of its September 1988 issue under the headline "Good Service Is Good Business." *The Pilot's Log*, a quarterly published by The New England for the edification of its agents, devoted the entire summer 1988 issue to the same theme under the banner "Carrying the Torch for Your Client." *The Pilot's Log* issue was published to coincide with the 1988 summer Olympic games in Seoul. Its editor took full advantage of the occasion, employing with abandon the athletic metaphors favored in the personal sales industry. The marathon runner bearing the torch of the Olympic games is featured on the magazine cover with the caption: "Agents Can Win the Gold with Needs Selling and Persistency." As noted in chapter 2, "persistency" refers to the agent's responsibility to make sure that the client develops the habits necessary to keep a financial security plan in force. The most important habit is, of course, the regular payment of required premiums.

74. Following Alfred Schutz, social theory articulates this distinction as a difference between actors' experience of their life-world and theoretical reflection on this life-world. The former is situated in a domain of practice and is determined by the pragmatics of the life-world itself and the situation of actors within it—in this case, the work world of agents and the contingencies of their occupational lives. The latter is situated in a domain of theory and is determined by the paradigms of a scientific discipline. See Alfred Schutz, *The Phenomenology of the Social World*, translated by George Walsh and Frederick Lehnert (Evanston, IL: Northwestern University Press), and "Common-Sense and the Scientific Interpretation of Human Action," pp. 3–47 in *Collected Papers I*, edited by Maurice Natanson (The Hague: Martinus Nijhoff, 1962).

75. The general point at issue here is elaborated by Peter Winch in his critique of Evans-Pritchard's famous account of Zande witchcraft. See Peter Winch, "Understanding a Primitive Society," pp. 78–111 in Bryan Wilson (ed.), *Rationality* (Oxford: Blackwell, 1970), and E. E. Evans-Pritchard, *Witchcraft, Oracles and Magic among the Azande* (Oxford: Clarendon Press, 1937). Evans-Pritchard explains Zande witchcraft as an internally inconsistent system of theoretical beliefs about the world. In response to this analysis, Winch raises two objections. First, Zande witchcraft cannot be understood as a theoretical system by means of which the Zande attempt to achieve a "quasi-scientific understanding of the world." Second, it is the Occidental social scientist, Evans-Pritchard, "obsessed with pressing Zande thought where it would not go—to a contradiction—who is guilty of misunderstanding, not the Zande" (Winch, "Understanding a Primitive Society," p. 93). For an argument along the same lines, cast in more concrete terms, see Mary Douglas, *Purity and Danger* (London: Routledge & Kegan Paul, 1984), pp. 89–91. Winch's argument

borrows liberally from Wittgenstein's analysis of contradiction and inconsistency. See especially Ludwig Wittgenstein, *Remarks on the Foundations of Mathematics*, edited by G. H. von Wright, R. Rhees, and G. E. M. Anscombe and translated by G. E. M. Anscombe (Cambridge, MA: The MIT Press, 1978). See also Wittgenstein's discussion of the concepts of a practice and a form of life in his *Philosophical Investigations*, translated by G. E. M. Anscombe (New York: Macmillan, 1953).

76. The general point at issue here concerning the limits of theoretical criticism and refutation was made by Wittgenstein in his "Remarks on Frazer's *The Golden Bough*," pp. 61–81 in C. G. Luckhardt (ed.), *Wittgenstein: Sources and Perspectives* (Ithaca, NY: Cornell University Press, 1979), and before him by Heinrich Rickert. Rickert's work in this area has not been translated into English. See his *System der Philosophie* (Tübingen: Mohr, 1921) and Guy Oakes, *Weber and Rickert: Concept Formation in the Cultural Sciences* (Cambridge, MA: The MIT Press, 1988), pp. 136–44.

77. Max Weber, "Politics as a Vocation," p. 123 in *From Max Weber: Essays in Sociology*.

78. The increasing autonomy of the various axiological and institutional spheres of life, their progressive isolation from one another, and the conflicts between them that are produced by this development form one of the principal motifs of Weber's *Economy and Society*. On the respects in which commerce follows its own rules and comes into conflict with the value spheres of ethics and religion, see *Economy and Society*, p. 585. On the inner dynamic of the development of the state and its conflicts with personal values, see p. 600. On the tensions between the autonomous value spheres of sexuality and religious ethics, eroticism and religious ethics, and art and religious ethics, see pp. 604–10. On the increasing autonomy of law—based on "a blind desire for logical consistency" and "the needs of the uninhibited intellectualism of scholars"—see p. 789. On the inner dynamic of urban development, see p. 1309.

79. On the company conventions held by direct selling organizations as rituals of recognition, see Biggart, *Charismatic Capitalism*, pp. 126–27.

80. Agents are not uniformly enthusiastic in their assessment of convention speakers, especially when speakers fail to conceal their own pecuniary motives and their intent to profit from the audience. One agent offers the following observations.

> At a convention a few years ago, the company brought in this consultant N [a name known to everyone in the life insurance industry]. This guy is an utterly shameless individual. He gets up and before he even starts, he tells you that in the back of the room you're gonna buy all this stuff. It's very expensive: tapes, charts, things you can use to manage your own time and essentially be like him. He gets up and tells you how to sell a lot more insurance, like he did. These people are taken very seriously by insurance salesmen, because they think they can be like him. Of course, they can't be. And who knows the real story behind super salesmen and consultants like N? But for whatever reason, they make millions, and a lot of it comes from agents who buy their material.

Index